SARAH PALIN'S
EXPERT GUIDE TO
GOOD GRAMMAR

SARAH PALIN'S EXPERT GUIDE TO GOOD GRAMMAR

WHAT YOU CAN LEARN FROM SOMEONE WHO DOESN'T KNOW RIGHT FROM WRITE

JENNY BARANICK

Skyhorse Publishing

Skyhorse Publishing books may be purchased in bulk at special discounts for sales promotion, corporate gifts, fund-raising, or educational purposes. Special editions can also be created to specifications. For details, contact the Special Sales Department, Skyhorse Publishing, 307 West 36th Street, 11th Floor, New York, NY 10018 or info@skyhorsepublishing.com.

Skyhorse® and Skyhorse Publishing® are registered trademarks of Skyhorse Publishing, Inc.®, a Delaware corporation.

Visit our website at www.skyhorsepublishing.com.

10 9 8 7 6 5 4 3 2 1

Library of Congress Cataloging-in-Publication Data is available on file.

Cover design by Rain Saukas
Cover photograph by iStock
Author photograph by Owen Ela

Print ISBN: 978-1-5107-1721-3
Ebook ISBN: 978-1-5107-1723-7

Printed in the United States of America

Table of Contents

Introduction

Material Girl

teach English at a fashion college. In other words, my students have no idea why they have to take my class, nor do they *want* to take my class. They signed up to explore the world of fabric and sketches, not commas and semicolons. Therefore, on the first day of class, I go in for the hard sell. I tell them that unless they learn how to write clearly and concisely, they will be doomed to a future of styling their childhood Barbie doll instead of styling Taylor Swift for the Grammys. I tell them that if they don't learn how to properly employ a comma or structure a sentence, the only line they will play a role in creating is the one in front of the unemployment office.

Okay, I'm not that harsh, but I do remind my students that until they do actually become the next Chanel and can afford to hire someone to write their website copy, e-mails, and Facebook posts, they need to learn to communicate clearly, concisely, and coherently. They need to support their points with concrete, specific examples to prove that they are knowledgeable. They need to learn proper grammar because it is often used as a barometer to measure intelligence and attention to detail, and they're going to need to convey those characteristics in their cover letters and résumés. Basically, I let them know that if they don't learn to communicate clearly, concisely, coherently, concretely, and correctly, they can't hope to amount to much— just, perhaps, the 2008 vice presidential candidate of the United States of America.

As an English teacher, I was so relieved that Sarah Palin wasn't going to be, as they say, one heartbeat away from the presidency. I don't want this book to be political (but, in full disclosure, I'm an English teacher who drives a Prius, listens to NPR, and whose celebrity crush is Jon Stewart, so you do the math), so I want to focus on the fact that I didn't want the person who was a heartbeat away from the presidency to be someone whose grammar gave me heart palpitations—just like I'm sure a history teacher would be relieved not to have a vice president who believed that Paul Revere was warning the British, or a geography teacher would be relieved not to have a vice president who mixed up North Korea and South Korea, or a science teacher would be relieved to not have a vice president that didn't agree with 97 percent of scientists.

Sarah Palin certainly didn't disappear into obscurity following her ticket's defeat, but after 2008 I lost track of her. We traveled in different circles. While she and her family were on TV killing Caribou on Sunday nights, I was watching *Mad Men*. While she was at her Tea Party, I was having coffee. While she was opining on Fox News, I was not even aware that she was doing that because I don't watch Fox News. But then, in January of 2016, I saw a clip of her insane Donald Trump endorsement speech on Stephen Colbert, and I just had to YouTube it and see it in its entirety.

Sentences that defy the rules of the elite grammar establishment, statements that refuse to bloat the economy of the sentence by bending over and kowtowing to concrete details, the moose in headlights look on Donald Trump's face— I laughed to myself, yep, that's classic Sarah Palin. But then a familiar feeling came over me. It was the same feeling that I get when I read my students' final essays only to find that they neglected to incorporate any of the feedback I provided them throughout the course. I should be used to it by now, but I can never help feeling disappointed in an indifference to improving. It's not like I expected Sarah's language to have gone through an Eliza Doolittle-sized transformation (the blizzard in Wasilla stays mainly in the . . . yeah, it doesn't work). And it's not that I don't recognize that her communication style is effective on many levels. But since

2008, she has been repeatedly lambasted in the media for her rambling, incoherent speeches and for her "struggle with the English language." It's been over eight years since she stepped onto the national stage and become a household name; why hasn't she even tried to improve?

I have a few theories:

Theory #1: She doesn't struggle with English; she speaks American.

When Palin told Jake Tapper in a CNN interview that immigrants who come to the US should "speak American," I assumed she had simply made another of her infamous blunders and meant to say "English"— but maybe not. Maybe Sarah Palin is so patriotic that she created her own American language.

In her autobiography, *Going Rogue: An American Life*, Palin described the Alaskan State Fair as a perfect depiction of "small-town America," and I realized that she speaks a lot like the scene she described. She mentioned the cotton candy, and her sentences, much like cotton candy, tend to be a lot of fluff and little substance. She also mentioned the footlong hotdogs, and like hotdogs are made up of disparate body parts, her sentences are made up of unrelated phrases. For example:

> And all these new Democrat voters that are going to be coming on over border as we keep the borders open, and bequeathing our children millions in new debt, and refusing to fight back for our solvency and our sovereignty, even though that's why we elected them and sent them as a majority to D.C.

We start with Democrat voters who haven't even crossed the border yet. We've got them bequeathing our children millions in debt. Now, we've got them refusing to fight back for our solvency and sovereignty, but why would they fight for our solvency and sovereignty? They're not even from here. And after all that, after they put our kids in debt and refuse to fight for us, it turns out we elected them and sent them to D.C.

Either we make terrible choices or that's a two-foot-long hotdog.

Theory #2: She's a Maverick.

I capitalized "Maverick" because I don't mean "maverick" in the way that Palin repeatedly described herself and John McCain during the 2008 campaign. I'm referring to the character that Tom Cruise portrayed in *Top Gun* who famously felt the need, the need for speed. In other words, maybe Palin did some speed right before giving her endorsement speech. A sober person wouldn't use the phrase "suck off" in a speech to endorse a candidate, right?

Theory #3: It doesn't matter

It was widely speculated that Palin's teleprompter went down during her Iowa Freedom Summit speech. Why? Because these words came out of her mouth:

> For it is they who point a finger not realizing that they have triple the amount of fingers pointin' right back at 'em.

And these:

> By the way, uh, you know, the man can only ride ya' when your back is bent, so strengthen it. Then the man can't ride ya'.

When Sean Hannity asked her if her teleprompter did, in fact, go down and if she had any trouble with her speech, she responded by pointing out that she received a standing ovation during and after the speech. And she did!

If an incoherent, rambling speech receives a standing ovation, am I lying to my students about the need to communicate clearly and concisely and coherently and correctly? Is it time for me to put down the red pen and put on the red Naughty Monkey heels?

I don't think so. And I'm not just saying that because I don't want to look for another job and because I can't walk in heels; I'm saying that because of the speech Sarah Palin gave at the Republican National Convention when she accepted the vice presidential nomination. Thanks to that speech, John

McCain took the lead in the polls for the first time during the election. Thanks to that speech, the number of McCain backers who claimed to be enthusiastic about their candidate doubled. And it wasn't a rambling, incoherent, grammatically questionable speech. It was, even according to Palin's opponent, Joe Biden, a "well-crafted" speech. It was a speech that White House speechwriter Jon Favreau said that although "it seems silly to think about now" he remembers watching "and was scared of Sarah Palin as the vice presidential nominee." Sure, Palin didn't write it, but the fact is that the words that she delivered made a difference; they changed people's minds, they convinced people that she was qualified. The speeches that she has given since then, the rambling incoherent ones, ignite a few loyal fans—but I doubt they turn any nonbelievers into believers.

We write cover letters and résumés to convince someone who has never met us to hire us. We write web copy to sell our products and services to strangers. We write business plans to persuade investors to part with their money. We write proposals to compete for jobs. We write e-mails to colleagues whose inboxes are cluttered with unread messages. We write Facebook posts to elicit as many "likes" as possible to boost our self-esteem. We need our writing to convert nonbelievers into believers! Can I get a Hallelujah?

Speaking of believers, Stephen Colbert is one. He was so excited to have Sarah Palin back in the spotlight following her Trump endorsement speech, he exclaimed, "God, I have missed you. It's like a magical eagle made a wish on a flag pin and it came to life. Which is great. For me." It was great for him because, as he explained, that although Trump gave him material to work with on his show, "Nobody compares to the original material girl." And what can I say? Colbert's enthusiasm was contagious. I checked out some of Palin's material, and Colbert was right: in order to emulate much of it, one would have to tase the part of the brain that understands sentence structure. But as a teacher, I knew what I had to do. I had to turn it into a teachable moment. I hope you enjoy and learn from these writing lessons gleaned from the words of Sarah Louise Palin.

Chapter 1

Sentence Fragments: A Bridge to Nowhere

On November 4, 2008, John McCain and Sarah Palin lost their bid for the presidency. Nine months later, Rush Limbaugh lost ninety pounds. Coincidence?

Mere days before the election, in an interview with the *London Telegraph*, Limbaugh revealed that his gut hadn't been giving him any indication of the race's outcome. "But," he said, "it started talking to me last night." And what it told him was that McCain and Palin were going to win. Clearly, Limbaugh got rid of his gut out of anger for the lies it told him.

But let's imagine for a moment that Rush Limbaugh's gut had been correct and Sarah Palin had been elected as vice president. As we all know, as vice president, Sarah Palin would have been one heartbeat away from the presidency—and, heaven forbid, if something had happened to John McCain, a Palin presidency would certainly have changed the landscape of America—literally. We would have had to hire a bunch of cartographers to relocate New Hampshire to the Northwest on the US map. We would also have had to revamp our foreign policy so we could "stand with our North Korean allies." In addition, we would have had to rewrite our history books to recount that Paul Revere was actually warning the British, not the Americans. And then after all of that trouble, Sarah probably would have just quit anyway.

You see, Sarah seems to have of pattern of failing to complete the jobs she starts. She resigned from her job as chairwoman of the Alaska Oil and Gas Conservation Commission. She resigned from her job as Alaska's governor. And she shut down her subscription-based online channel after less than a year. (Even her "Moose Meat: It's What's for Dinner" segment couldn't save it.) So I guess it should come as no surprise that she also fails to complete many of her sentences.

But here's the thing about Sarah Palin: quitting works for her. Leaving the Alaska Oil and Gas Conservation Commission helped propel her into the governorship. And resigning as governor enabled her to pursue a 7 million dollar book deal, 100, 000 dollar speaking fees, and a 250,000 dollar per episode reality show deal (because the one thing the Kardashians don't do on national TV is shoot caribou). But does failing to complete her sentences also work in Palin's favor?

Before we have a look at Palin's incomplete sentences, also known as sentence fragments, let's discuss the components that make up complete sentences. This will help us identify when a sentence is not complete. I know that, unlike Sarah, most of you do, in fact, finish what you start, including your sentences. But like there is more than one way to skin a caribou, there is more than one way to express a complete sentence— some of which are often mistaken for fragments.

A complete sentence fulfills three criteria:

1. It contains a subject (the person, place, thing, or idea the sentence is about).
2. It contains a verb (the word that conveys the subject's action or state of being).
3. It completes a thought.

To explore complete sentences further, let's examine what it looks like when Sarah Palin actually finishes the sentences she starts:

- Only dead fish go with the flow.

This sentence contains a subject: "fish." It contains a verb: the action verb "go." It completes a thought: Upon finishing the sentence, we get that dead fish are the only ones that go with the flow.

And, no, this sentence is not part of an Alaskan fishing lesson; it's a metaphor Palin used in her resignation speech to explain why she was quitting the governorship.

- Buck up or get in the truck.

It might seem as though this sentence doesn't have a subject, but like the alleged Bumpit Sarah inserts to achieve that perfect hillock of hair on the top of her head, just because you can't see it, it doesn't mean it's not there doing a fabulous job. This is an imperative sentence, a sentence that gives a command, and the subject of all imperative sentences is an invisible "you."

That's right, YOU buck up or get in the truck. No more pussyfootin' around!

- They are also building schools for the Afghan children so that there is hope and opportunity in our neighboring country of Afghanistan.

The subject of this sentence is "they." And we know what *they* are doing; they "are building," which is a helping verb. In this case, "are" joins with "building" to help convey that the building is ongoing. And it completes a thought: the sentence expresses whom "they" are building schools for (the Afghan children) and it even explains why (so that there is hope and opportunity in our neighboring country of Afghanistan).

What the sentence doesn't explain is when Afghanistan moved into our neighborhood. I wish I would have known. I would have brought them over a welcome basket.

- As Putin rears his head and comes into the airspace of the United States of America, where—where do they go?

It might seem as though "Putin" is the subject of this sentence and that the verb is "rears," but do not be fooled by Putin and his rearing head. The phrase "As Putin rears his head and comes into the airspace of the United States of America" is a subordinate clause. A subordinate clause sets the stage for the actual sentence, but it can't stand alone as a sentence. Say it out loud. It doesn't complete a thought, right? But it does set the stage, and on the stage is Putin's head smack dab in the middle of America's airspace. Now comes the actual complete sentence: "Where do they go?"

Because it can be difficult to identify subjects and verbs in a question, it's helpful to turn the sentence into a statement. The statement will sound "backasswards," as Sarah would say, but it works. The statement form of this question is "They do go where" (See? Backassward). The subject is the pronoun "they," which in this case is a pronoun that refers back to Putin (which is incorrect because "Putin" is singular and "they" is plural—but that's a lesson for a different chapter). The verb is the helping verb "do go." And this sentence completes a thought: Where does Putin go when he rears his head and comes into US airspace?

My guess is Putin's head heads straight to visit his good buddy Steven Seagal.

- I am not one to be a word police.

First of all, Sarah, we know. Hiring Sarah as a member of the word police would make as much sense as hiring Nixon as a member of the ethics commission. But I included this sentence because it contains the last of the three types of verbs: a linking verb. A linking verb does not express an action. Instead, it conveys a state of being by connecting the subject to additional information about the subject, such as a description. The most common linking verbs are forms of the verb "to be" (e.g., is, was, were, are). In this sentence *I* is the subject, "am" is the verb, and it connects the subject to a description of the subject ("not a word police"), thereby completing a thought.

Therefore, it cannot be "refudiated" that it is a complete sentence.

- *I'm here to support the next president of the United States, Donald Trump.*

I included this complete sentence for the horror fans out there, because this is one of the scariest complete sentences I have ever encountered.

And now let's look at Sarah Palin's incomplete sentences. When it comes to her sentence fragments, Sarah Palin is a dead fish. By that I mean that she goes with the flow. And by that I mean she tends to create the same kinds of fragments that most of us do.

- A new commander-in-chief who will never leave our men behind.

This is a relative clause fragment. If you're not into elitist grammar jargon, as I suspect some ex-governors of Alaska are not, you can think of a relative clause fragment as one that contains "who," "whose," "which," or "that."

There seems to be a subject, "commander-in-chief," and a verb, "will leave," but that doggarnit "who" prevents it from completing a thought. If we take out the "who," we have a complete thought. The subject is "commander-in-chief," the verb is "will leave," and the complete thought is that this commander-in-chief will never leave our men behind.

Having said that, I am not suggesting we leave the "who" out. That would change the meaning. We'll discuss how to deal with these types of fragments later when we see them in context, but for now we're just identifying them. As Palin said, it's important to "first to recognize who the enemy is and to be candid enough and honest enough to let the people know." Well, here you go, people, a fragment has reared its ugly head into our airspace.

- Because that's what's going to let you make America great again.

This is a dependent clause fragment, or you can think of it as the type of fragment responsible for your English teacher telling you never to start a sentence with the word "because." The truth is that it is grammatically correct to start sentences with "because," but because we tend to leave such sentences as fragments, English teachers often just tell us to avoid them.

It's similar to why John McCain's aides told Sarah Palin to avoid calling Biden by his last name in the vice presidential debates. She kept referring to him as O'Biden during the prep sessions, so instead of making sure that she learned how to pronounce it correctly, they gave up and told her to just ask him if she could call him Joe.

- To make things great again.

This is an infinitive phrase fragment. An infinitive is the *to* form of a verb (i.e., She likes *to shoot* wolves from planes. She wants *to drill*, baby, drill). "To make things great again" contains the verb "to make," but it lacks a subject. Who does she believe is going to make things great again?

I'll give you a hint: he and a famous Disney duck share the same name and a proneness to temper tantrums when things don't go their way.

- PETA barking their tired old death threats against us, and I'm thinkin' oh get in line.

This is a gerund fragment, also known as an *ing* fragment, which is probably the most common fragment. Its popularity probably stems from the fact that people mistake the gerund (the *ing* word) for a verb. But a gerund is not a verb. It's actually a verb turned into a noun. It's kind of like when you put lipstick on a bulldog, you get a hockey mom. When you put an *ing* on the end of a verb, you get a noun.

Therefore, in the fragment above, PETA is the subject, but there's no verb. If Sarah would have called in reinforcements and employed the helping verb "was" and placed it before the "barking," she would have been in business.

But I guess she has bigger problems to worry about. PETA's about to go rogue and kill itself a mama grizzly.

- Steve very strong.

I call this a WTF, a Weird Tarzan Fragment.

So, yes, Sarah Palin often communicates in incomplete sentences, but let's get back to the question I posed at the beginning of this chapter: Does not completing her sentences work in her favor? To answer that question, let's look at a couple of her fragments in context:

> Thank a vet, and know that the United States military deserves a commander-in-chief that loves our country passionately, and will never apologize for this country. **A new commander-in-chief who will never leave our men behind. A new commander-in-chief, one who will never lie to the families of the fallen.**

In context, these fragments actually work. Although we have most likely been taught in English class to avoid fragments, when used sparingly, fragments can enhance our writing and speaking. In this case, using fragments varies the rhythm of Palin's speech, making it punchier than it would have been had she completed the last two sentences. Let's have a look at what happens when we turn those last two fragments into complete sentences:

> Thank a vet, and know that the United States military deserves a commander-in-chief that loves our country passionately, and will never apologize for this country. **They deserve a new commander-in-chief who will never leave our men behind. They deserve a new commander-in-chief, one who will never lie to the families of the fallen.**

The sentences are heavier making the delivery less vigorous. Also, notice how adding "they deserve" weakens the emphasis on "commander-in-chief."

It's as if the words "they deserve" form a great, inexpensive wall that obstructs our view of the commander-in-chief.

Here's another fragment in context:

His power, his [Trump's] passion is the fabric of America and it's woven by work ethic and dreams and drive and faith in the Almighty. **What a combination.** Are you ready to share in that again, Iowa?

Again, in this context this fragment works. *What a combination* is zippier and more emphatic than saying something like "Those characteristics are quite a combination." Also, using a short, punchy fragment following the long sentence that comes before it varies the paragraph's rhythm, making it more compelling.

Let's take a moment, though, to imagine an America that is woven by the fabric of Donald Trump's passion. Is it just me, or are you envisioning the fabric as gold lamé too?

However, not all of Sarah Palin's fragments effectively provide emphasis and variety. Some of them are like Alaskan winters: long, blustery, and disorienting. The following excerpts look like complete sentences—in fact, they're so long they look like they might even be run-ons—but even though they contain many thoughts, not one thought is completed.

Let me ask you, why is it, considering how fast the world is spinning, and world-changing events that go on all over the globe that affect our lives, world-changing events, thousands of them every day, why do you suppose that the same big three, supposedly competing networks, that have virtually the same news content every night.

And Secretary Rice, having recently met with leaders on one side or the other, there, also, still in these waning days of the Bush administration, trying to forge that peace, and that needs to be done, and that will be the top of an agenda item, also, under a McCain-Palin administration.

And he, who would negotiate deals, kind of with the skills of a community organizer maybe organizing a neighborhood tea, well, he deciding that, 'No, America would apologize' and as part of the deal, as the enemy sends a message to the rest of the world that they capture and we kowtow and we apologize, and then, we bend over and say, 'Thank you, enemy.'

So to answer the question posed at the beginning of this chapter about whether or not failing to complete her sentences works for Sarah Palin, the answer is . . . sometimes.

We can use fragments for emphasis and variety, but we should use them sparingly and carefully. Complete sentences exist for a reason. As Harvard University instructor Constance Hale explains, "the best sentences bolt a clear subject to a dramatic predicate, making a mini-narrative. The drama makes us pay attention."

As we can see from the examples of Palin's long, dizzying fragments, they don't take us on dramatic journey. Instead, they take us on a bridge to nowhere.

Chapter 2

Dangling Participles: The Bard

"High risk, high reward." That's how A. B. Culvahouse, the lawyer who vetted Palin as McCain's running mate, described Palin. Palin, on the other hand, played much safer odds when choosing her right-hand woman. To help her write *Going Rogue: An American Life,* she chose Lynn Vincent, a bestselling ghostwriter. But in addition to Vincent's success, Palin surely chose Vincent because the other books Vincent co-wrote share *Going Rogue's* conservative, Christian themes. There is one thing, however, that *Going Rogue* does not share with all other of the books that Lynn Vincent ghostwrote: Lynn Vincent's name on the cover.

Vincent signed a nondisclosure agreement, so she's legally bound to keep her mouth shut about how things went down with Palin, but clearly she's pissed. When asked in a writing workshop about how ghostwriters are given credit, Vincent said, "With Sarah Palin, it was, like, 'Thanks, Lynn Vincent, for taking out the trash.'" Perhaps that's because Vincent was also barely acknowledged in *Going Rogue's* Acknowledgements section. The first person that Palin acknowledges is, of course, herself. "I'm very glad this writing exercise is over," she writes. "I love to write, but not about myself. I'm thankful now to have kept journals about Alaska and my friends and family ever since I was a little girl." Then, after she lets the readers know that she hated writing the book they just read and applauds herself for diligently documenting her life, she thanks another thirty-seven people (one whose name is Happy) until she finally gets to Vincent. She writes, "Thanks, as well, to Lynn Vincent for her indispensible help in getting the words on paper." "Getting the words on paper" makes it sound like Vincent's job was merely to take dictation. But if I were Vincent, it would be the dismissive "as well" that really turned the knife.

Clearly, Palin is embarrassed that she needed help writing the autobiography. But she shouldn't be. Her specialty isn't prose; it's poetry. And as a poet, she experiments with all genres. The *New Republic* dubbed her the Walt Whitman of Wasilla for this Whitman-like "free-flowing democratic verse":

> Turning safety nets into hammocks, and all these new
> Democrat voters that are going to be coming on over the
> border as we keep the borders open.
> How 'bout the rest of us?
> Right wingin', bitter clingin', proud
> clingers of our guns, our god, and our religions,
> and our Constitution.
> Tell us that we're not red enough?

Slate pointed out that she also dabbles in haikus:

> These corporations.
> Today it was AIG,
> Important call, there.

In her Trump endorsement, she showed off her rhyming prowess:

> Well, look, we are mad,
> and we've been had.

And this excerpt from her Conservative Political Action Conference (CPAC) speech reveals her early inspirations:

> I do not like this Uncle Sam, I do not like his health care scam;
> I do not like these dirty crooks or how they lie and cook the books;
> I do not like when Congress steals, I do not like their crony deals;
> I do not like this buy-in man, I do not like 'oh yes we can.'

I think I've caught the bug. You don't mind if I express my points in poetry, do you?

> Clubbing a halibut on the head, Sarah Palin proves to be an ardent angler.
> Coining the word "refudiate," is she a word creator or mangler?
> Her rifle she proudly holds erect, but with her participles she's a dangler.

Ok, I'll keep my day job.

So what exactly does it mean that Sarah Palin dangles her participles? Well, let's look at a few examples from the bard, herself:

Looking around at all of you—you hardworking Iowa families, you farm families and teachers and teamsters and cops and cooks, you rockin' rollers and holy rollers, all of you who work so hard, you full-time moms, you with the hands that rock the cradle; you all make the world go round and now our cause is one.

A participial phrase is a phrase that begins with a word ending in *ing* or *ed*. In this example, it's the part of the sentence that I've put in bold. Now, what the participial phrase is *supposed* to do is refer to the subject of the sentence. But this one goes rogue. This participial phrase is referring to the person who is "looking around" at the farm families, teachers, teamsters, cops, cooks, et al., who, in this case, is Sarah Palin (with Trump standing by her side becoming increasingly uncomfortable). But the subject of the sentence is "you"—and by "you," she means the farm families, teachers, teamsters, et al. So basically she is saying that by looking around at themselves, they are making the world go around. I know; I'm getting dizzy just thinking about it. But that's what a dangling participle does; it disorients the reader because it's a participial phrase that loses track of its target, which is supposed to be the subject.

To avoid dangling, the subject of this sentence should be *I.* For example, it could look like this:

> **Looking around at all of you—you hardworking Iowa families, you farm families and teachers and teamsters and cops and cooks, you rockin' rollers and holy rollers, all of you who work so hard, you full-time moms, you with the hands that rock the cradle;** I see a group of Americans who make the world go around and now our cause is one.

But my real concern is that teachers are there in support of her.

On second thought, though, maybe Palin's dangling participles are not incorrect; maybe they're poetic. The dangling participle in the next example appears to be a grammatical metaphor for her feelings:

> **Calling GOP front-runner supporters "low information" disengaged voters,** Ted Cruz's insinuation reeks of all the reasons America knows "the status quo has got to go."

Again, the participial phrase is in bold and should technically refer to the subject of this sentence. The subject of this sentence is *insinuation*, but the participial phrase refers to Ted Cruz. Sure, it's Ted Cruz's insinuation, but it was actually Ted Cruz who was doing the calling, not the insinuation. A non-dangling version of this sentence would be the following:

> **Calling GOP front-runner supporters "low information" disengaged voters,** Ted Cruz makes an insinuation that reeks of all the reasons America knows the status quo has got to go.

13

But, as I said, before, perhaps Palin took poetic license in order to make sure that the form of this sentence (i.e., the dangling participle) mirrors the content of the sentence (i.e., her feelings about Ted Cruz). In 2012, Palin endorsed Cruz for Texas senator. Four years later, however, she left him dangling in order to support Trump. And what more poetic way to express that than through a dangling participle? Truly transformative stuff!

The following sentence doesn't technically contain a dangling participle. It contains its cousin: the dangling modifier. A dangling modifier is basically the same thing as a dangling participle—a descriptive phrase that incorrectly fails to target the subject— it just doesn't start with a word ending in "ing" or "ed." She dangles a modifier in an ode to Donald Trump:

And yes, as a multi-billionaire, we still root him on because he roots us on.

On second thought, is this a dangling modifier or is it the sentence that is responsible for earning her the nickname Walt Whitman of Wasilla? At first glance, I *thought* this was a dangling modifier because the descriptive phrase contains the singular "a multi-billionaire" and the subject of the sentence is the plural "we." I also assumed that by "a multi-billionaire" she was referring to Trump. But maybe she was just channeling Walt. In Walt Whitman's poem "Come, Said My Soul," he writes, "for we are one." Surely, Palin adopted this concept and used the singular "a multi-billionaire" to convey that we are really just one multi-billionaire. Because if we are one, that means our money is one, and surely if we pulled all our money, we'd be one multi-billionaire. Poetry truly does enrich our lives! I say we buy a yacht!

The irony is that most people would consider Sarah Palin a huntress shooting wolves from a plane rather than a poet shooting metaphors from her soul, but she is actually not as good a shot as you would expect from someone who says, "We eat, therefore we hunt." As shown on an episode of her reality show, it actually took Sarah quite a few shots to hit a caribou. In other words, she almost didn't eat. She shows similar marksmanship in the following "sentence." Her mouth shoots out participles, but they don't hit any targets:

> GOP majorities **handing** over a blank check to fund Obamacare and Planned Parenthood and illegal immigration that competes for your jobs and **turning** safety nets into hammocks and all these new Democrat voters that are **going** to be **coming** on over border as we keep the borders open, and **bequeathing** our children millions in new debt, and **refusing** to fight back for our solvency and our sovereignty, even though that's why we elected them and sent them as a majority to D.C.

The sheer multitude of participles has inspired me to write a haiku:

> These participles.
> Today it was ING,
> Erratic use, there.

Like poet e e cummings forewent the use of capital letters and poet Gertrude Stein omitted punctuation, it is very possible that poet Sarah Palin dangles her participles in adherence to the poetic tradition of breaking grammar convention. But for those of us not communicating through *ars poetica*, we should not dangle our participles. We should not dangle them in a box. We should not dangle them with a fox. We should not dangle them here or there. We should not dangle them anywhere.

Chapter 3

Agreement:
Going Rogue

M any book reviews claim that Sarah Palin's autobiography, *Going Rogue: An American Life*, was largely a vehicle for Sarah Palin to settle the score with her detractors. Thomas Frank from the *Wall Street Journal* wrote, "With an impressive attention to detail, Ms. Palin settles every score, answers every criticism; locates a scapegoat for every foul-up, and fastens an insult on every critic, down to the last obscure Palin-doubter back in Alaska." Thomas Frank has written several books, himself, but he was not an English major (he received his doctorate in history), so I'm not surprised that his review didn't include an appreciation for Palin's subtle use of literary devices.

On page 15 of Palin's tome, she shares a memory from her childhood. She doesn't reveal her exact age, but the context of this excerpt seems to place her in kindergarten:

Leaning on Mom's shoulder in the pew at Church on the Wild-wood during a Sunday sermon, I heard the pastor use the word 'different.' 'I can spell different!' I excitedly whispered in her ear, and scribbled it in the margin of the church bulletin. It was my first big word, and I was proud to have figured it out myself. It was the first time Mom didn't give me her stern don't-talk-in-church look but instead smiled warmly and seemed as proud as I was.

The fact that at the age of five or six Sarah Heath (she wasn't married yet) could spell the word "different" might not seem that impressive considering a six-year-old Lori Anne Madison became the youngest National Spelling Bee contestant, citing "sprachgefuhl" as her favorite word to spell. But that's not really the point. What Palin is doing is foreshadowing, which is a literary device that hints at an important plot-point early in the story only to come back later in the story full bore. In other words, it's no accident that Sarah Heath's first big word was "different" because Sarah *is* different. The reader will find out later on in the book that she's, in fact, a maverick. As the title suggests, Sarah goes rogue.

The association between Sarah Palin and "going rogue" didn't originate from Sarah, herself; it came from a McCain aide—and it wasn't a compliment. Members of McCain's staff were getting frustrated with Palin's tendency to go off message. For example, she openly voiced her disagreement with the McCain campaign's decision to pull out of Michigan. And in *Going Rogue*, Palin makes it clear that it wasn't just the campaign's Michigan decision she disagreed with; she disagreed with just about everything and everyone on the campaign trail.

She disagreed with Steve Schmidt, McCain's campaign manager, about his choice to focus on the conflict in the Middle East "come hell or high water" when she felt the focus should have been on the economy. She disagreed with the "jaded aura" of the "professional political caste" that led them to smoke so much they "looked like a walking smoke cloud with legs." She disagreed with the people who thought she wore her hair in the famous updo because it made her look "chic." "Nah," she claimed, "it just saves me a few minutes every morning to plop it on top of my head." She disagreed with the campaign's decision to have Katie Couric, "the lowest-rated news anchor in network television," interview her. (Palin had recommended

FOX.) She disagreed with the McCain staff's method of prepping her for the vice presidential debate. "Just let me answer the question, dang it," was a note she had scribbled in the margin of her debate notes. She disagreed with Steve Schmidt about his claim about "the importance of carbohydrates to cognitive connections and blah-blah-blah," especially because of his "rotund physique." She disagreed with the *Saturday Night Live* writers about what constitutes funny. When she saw the jokes they had created for her *SNL* appearance, she thought, "Nah. C'mon, New York talent, we can do better than that." And she disagreed with basic sanity when she said, "Ann Coulter was spot on."

Sarah Palin is clearly comfortable with disagreements. I might even go so far as to suggest that she enjoys them. In fact, she seems to enjoy them so much that sometimes she won't even let her subjects and verbs agree. And subjects and verbs are really only expected to agree on one thing: number. In other words, if the subject is singular, the verb is supposed to be singular too, and if the subject is plural, the verb is supposed to be plural. That's it! They don't have to agree about hair or diet or jokes or the sanity of a woman who said, "If we took away women's right to vote, we'd never have to worry about another Democrat president. It's kind of a pipe dream, it's a personal fantasy of mine, but I don't think it's going to happen."

Of course, many of us are not as comfortable with disagreements as Sarah is. We like it when our subjects and verbs get along, and Robert Schlesinger, the managing editor at the *U.S. News* website, seems to be one of those people. He was upset by a subject-verb disagreement in this excerpt from a fundraising e-mail sent by Sarah Palin:

> Thirty-seven Governorships, one third of the United States Senate, and the entire House of Representatives is up for election.

The disagreement exists because the subject of this sentence is plural—it contains three nouns—"Governorships," "Senate," and "House of Representatives"—but the verb is the singular "is." The verb should be "are." An amicable version of this sentence would read as follows:

Thirty-seven Governorships, one third of the United States Senate, and the entire House of Representatives are up for election.

But I'm not sure if the subject-verb disagreement in this particular sentence stems from Palin's penchant for disagreement or her passion for proximity. Having famously cited Alaska's proximity to Russia as evidence of her foreign relations experience, Sarah Palin clearly believes that juxtaposition is very, very powerful. Therefore, because "House of Representatives" is singular and "House of Representatives" is closest to the verb, perhaps Sarah felt that making the verb agree with its neighbor took precedence over grammatical correctness.

But Palin is not completely off base (about that). For example, proximity can play a role in subject-verb agreement. Had she written that only "One-third of the United States Senate is up for election," she would have been correct because when subjects contain fractions, percentages, and indefinite quantifiers, such as "all" and "some," the verb agrees in number with the preceding noun, not the fraction, percentage, or indefinite quantifier. In Palinese, that agreement rule would be that when a verb rears its head and comes into the air space of a subject that contains a fraction, percentage, or indefinite quantifier, the verb agrees in number with the preceding noun.

Palin may have exuded certainty about Alaska's proximity, but she wasn't as confident about Alaska's positioning—which may be responsible for her next subject-verb agreement error. In September of 2008, Palin said she wished that Alaska "could be recognized as the head and not the tail of the US" when just months before that she said the following:

There's been so many words, Ed, over the state of Alaska, we being the head and not the tail . . .

It looks as if she doesn't know how to make heads or tails of whether Alaska is the head or the tail of the US, and similarly, she can't seem to make heads or tails of the subject in the sentence above. And that's because it's a special kind of sentence; it's a sentence that starts with "there." When a sentence starts with "there," the subject and the verb swap places. Traditionally, the subject is the head and the verb is the tail. In other words, the subject comes first and the verb follows it. But when "there" begins a sentence, the subject follows the verb. In this sentence, the subject is "words" and the verb is "has" (the *'s* part of "there's"). But "words" is plural and "has" is singular, so this is the grammatically correct version of the sentence:

> There have been so many words, Ed, over the state of Alaska, we being the head and not the tail . . .

Ed, do you agree?

I know that I claimed that the disagreements between Sarah Palin's subjects and verbs had to do with her fondness for confrontation, but the next instance of her subject-verb disagreement might actually have to do with basketball coach John Wooden. John Wooden wasn't Palin's basketball coach; he was a head coach at UCLA who is famous for his inspirational quotes. And clearly he inspired Palin because she included one of his quotes in *Going Rogue:* "Our land is everything to us . . . I will tell you one of the things we remember on our land. We remember our grandfathers paid for it – with their lives." Well, even though Palin attributed that quote to John Wooden, he didn't actually say that. It was actually Native American activist John Woodenlegs. But you can see how she might have gotten her Johns confused. But the fact that she did, at least, attempt to quote John Wooden means that she must be familiar with him, and he did say, "The true test of a man's character is what he does when no one is watching," which could very well be responsible for a subject-verb disagreement in this sentence:

> I can give you examples of things that John McCain **has done** that **has shown** his foresight, his pragmatism, and his leadership abilities.

Wooden's quote might be responsible for the subject-verb disagreement in this sentence because it claims that a man is what he does, and in this sentence Palin seems to conflate who John McCain, the man, is and what John McCain, the man, does. You'll see that she uses two singular verbs that begin with the helping verb "has": "has done" and "has shown." (I put them in bold.) The verb "has done" agrees with its subject, "John McCain." However, "John McCain" isn't the subject that performs the verb "has shown"; the subject that performs the verb "has shown" is "things," and "things" is plural. Therefore, the second "has" should be "have," like this:

> I can give you examples of things that John McCain **has done** that **have shown** his foresight, his pragmatism, and his leadership abilities.

Or maybe this subject-verb disagreement *was* a result of Palin's confrontational nature because she was channeling a quote from another John whose last name starts with "W," John Wayne: "When you stop fighting, that's death."

Here's the irony: the woman who in 2008 openly celebrated her fighting instincts by referring to herself as a pit bull wearing lipstick won the Miss Congeniality contest in a beauty pageant in 1984. Did twenty-four years of hard Alaska living toughen Sarah up? Nope. Even back in 1984, that pit bull was there. Sarah seemed to do everything she could to soothe the beast during the pageant—she even played the flute for the talent portion—but a little growl escaped during the question-and-answer portion. In *Going Rogue*, Palin recounts that she came across an old pageant video in which a judge (conveniently) asked her if a woman could be vice president. Palin claims to have answered, "Yes, I believe a woman could be vice president," which she claims to have (conveniently) followed by saying, "I believe a woman could be president." Then, the judge asked if Sarah Heath (she still wasn't married) would vote for a candidate just because she was a woman, and this is where the fangs came out, because in Sarah Heath's answer, her pronoun and antecedent did not agree:

> *No, I would not vote for someone just because they were a woman.*

A pronoun is a word that takes place of a noun (e.g., he, she, it, they, them, I, we, you), and the antecedent is the noun that it takes the place of. And, like a subject and verb, a pronoun and its antecedent must agree in number. In this sentence, the pronoun is "they," which is plural, but its antecedent, "someone," is singular. Therefore, the pronoun should be singular too, like this:

No, I would not vote for someone just because she was a woman.

We use the gender-specific pronoun "she" because, in this sentence, she was only referring to women.

But, of course, gender is not the only issue we should be concerned about when deciding whom to vote for; there's also the very important issue of thuggery as Ms. Palin explained:

[M]y concern is for the **GOP candidate** who wins this primary, as **they** go forward to face the Obama presidential ticket machine and really the thuggery that is involved in that.

If you ask me, this sentence is a bit thuggish because, again the pronoun and its antecedent don't agree. "GOP candidate" is singular, but the pronoun that refers to it, "they," is plural. But how we fix this particular error depends on what time of the day Palin uttered these words. Sarah Palin said this on FOX news on January 4, 2012, the same day that Michelle Bachman dropped out of the primary. Now, had Palin said this before Bachman dropped out, the "GOP candidate" could have either been male or female, so the pronoun should be changed thusly:

[M]y concern is for the **GOP candidate** who wins this primary, as **he or she** goes forward to face the Obama presidential ticket machine and really the thuggery that is involved in that.

However, had it been after Bachman dropped out, only males would have been left in the primary, so this version would have been correct:

[M]y concern is for the **GOP candidate** who wins this primary, as **he** goes forward to face the Obama presidential ticket machine and really the thuggery that is involved in that.

Either way, it's so much better when our pronouns and antecedents get along, isn't it? Sentences should adopt the philosophy of "hugs not thugs."

But as much as Palin is a pit bull most of the year, even she can't resist the good tidings and the great joy of the Christmas holiday—so much so that she wrote a book called *Good Tidings and Great Joy: Protecting the Heart of Christmas.* And in the Christmas spirit, this book includes collective nouns, nouns that bring people and things together as one (e.g., team, family, audience, herd). Because collective nouns are made up of more than one entity (i.e., a herd of moose is made up of more than one moose), there's often confusion about whether or not collective nouns are singular or plural, and, consequently whether they require a singular or plural pronoun to take their place. And, well, it is confusing. Let's examine one of the collective nouns Palin uses in this excerpt from her Christmas book to get to the heart of the matter—and protect it:

> Without faith, we'd be, well, the secular Left — a **group** that data shows to be notoriously stingy with **their** time, money, and pleasant attitudes, and that **believes** "compassion" is best represented by a failed welfare state that traps millions in lifelong poverty and despair.

The collective noun we will be dealing with from this excerpt is "group," and it's clear that Palin is confused about whether or not it's singular or plural because she uses the plural pronoun "their" to take its place but she also pairs it with the singular verb "believes." A collective noun, like "group," is singular if the people or things that make it up are acting as a unified body, and it's plural if its members are acting individually. The "group" in question in this excerpt is the secular Left, and what they are doing is believing that "compassion" is best represented by a failed welfare state that traps millions in lifelong poverty and despair, which they obviously have plenty of time to do because they're not using that time spreading money, time, and pleasant attitudes. In this case, "group" is singular because she's discussing them as a unified whole—they all share the same belief. "Group" would have been considered plural if she had written something like "The group set 'compassion' traps in front of their homes in an effort to trap millions in lifelong poverty and despair." Because not all members of the secular Left group live in the same home, they would be setting the traps individually.

Sarah effectively used foreshadowing in *Going Rogue: An American Life* to let the reader know that the rogue behaviour was coming. And she showed us in the book how her rogue behavior could be manifested as it came back in plot point after plot point, after plot point, after plot point. And Palin used another literary device, denouement, which is a work's final resolution, so the audience would know what was next for Palin and her family. In the book's final paragraph, she said that first she was going to head back to "that kitchen table" in Alaska where she and her family would discuss the day's news and their next stop. The day's news, I'm assuming was going to come from any of the publications that came in front of them. Then, she and her family would travel down their next road because, as she always told her kids, "God doesn't drive parked cars." (But I have to ask, does anyone drive parked cars?) And then, she writes, "I'll pull out a road map—I want to show Piper the way to Michigan." In other words, she's going to teach Piper to follow in her roguish footsteps. So to Piper's future English teachers, expect Piper's subjects and verbs and pronouns and antecedents to disagree.

Chapter 4

Active Voice or Passive Voice: An Energetic Debate

S arah Palin was full of energy during her first TV interview as McCain's running mate. By full of energy, I don't mean she was exuding peppiness or the weird manic energy from Donald Trump's endorsement speech; I mean she would not stop talking about energy.

When Charlie Gibson introduced the interview, he explained that the focus would be national security, and accordingly asked Palin if the fact that she had commanded the National Guard and lived so close to Russia were sufficient security credentials. Palin answered, "Let me speak specifically about a credential that I do bring to this table, Charlie, and that's with energy independence." She continued with an explanation about how becoming energy independent would make the U.S. safer. Gibson countered with some basic math: "We consume, Governor, 25 percent of the world's energy and we have three percent of the world's natural resources." Palin acknowledged that energy independence wouldn't happen overnight and would take an "all-together approach."

So they cleared that up and then moved onto other issues concerning national security. Wrong! Gibson tried. He said, "National security is a lot more than energy." But Palin refused to let her energy dwindle. "But, Charlie," she replied, "there is an inherent link between energy and national security." Gibson repeated his former point: "I know, I'm just saying that national security is a whole lot more than energy." But Palin wouldn't diffuse her energy. "It is," she said, "but I want you to not lose sight of the fact that energy is a foundation of national security. It's that important. It's that significant." Gibson realized he'd have to change tactics and asked, "Did you ever travel outside the country prior to your trip to Kuwait and Germany last year?"

But if you don't mind, I'm going to pull a Sarah and get back to energy for a second. When Palin told Gibson they needed an "all-together approach," she explained that she was not just talking about petroleum and hydrocarbon; she was talking about alternative energy projects, conservation, and weatherization. What she didn't include as part of her approach was using active voice. The CNN analysis of the 2008 Vice Presidential Debate clarifies why active voice did not make it onto Sarah's list: she doesn't seem to be aware of the energy it can produce. CNN found that in the debate Palin used the passive voice in 8 percent of her sentences while Biden used passive voice in only 5 percent of his, and sentences expressed in the passive voice tend to be far less energetic than those written in the active. Let's check out active and passive voice in action by examining a couple of Palin's sentences about her desire to be appointed Secretary of Energy if Trump wins the election. First, she said this:

I think a lot about the Department of Energy, because energy is my baby: oil and gas and minerals, those things that God has dumped on this part of the Earth for mankind's use.

And right after, she said this:

If I were head of [the Department of Energy], I'd get rid of it.

Typical Palin. She hates being tied down by a job. But at least both of these sentences about energy are in active voice. Active voice means the subject performs the action. In the first sentence, the subject of the sentence, "I," performs the verb, "think." Also, the subject in the clause, "God," performs the verb, "has dumped." And in the second sentence, the subject, "I," performs the verb, "would get."

Now let's change these to passive voice. Passive voice is when the subject is acted upon.

> The Department of Energy is thought about a lot by me, because energy is my baby: oil and gas and minerals, those that have been dumped on this part of the Earth for mankind's use by God.

> If I were head of [the Department of Energy], it would be gotten rid of by me.

In the first sentence, the subject, "Department of Energy," is not performing the action (i.e., doing the thinking). It is receiving the action; it is being thought about. Also, in the clause in the second half of the sentence, the oil and gas and minerals aren't performing the dumping; they are receiving the dumping. And in the second sentence, the subject "it," isn't performing the action (i.e., doing the getting rid of); it's on the receiving end of the action; it's being gotten rid of. By comparing the passive and active constructions of these sentences, it's clear that active voice tends to be, as Strunk and White (who are like the Founding Fathers of grammar) explained, more "direct and vigorous" than the passive. And Stephen King really hates the passive voice. He said, "It's weak, it's circuitous, and it's frequently tortuous."

But many people find Palin's voice circuitous and frequently tortuous yet she still has her supporters, and so it is with the passive voice. Linguist Steven Pinker points out, "No construction [i.e., the passive voice] could have survived for millennia if it did not serve a purpose." And writer Constance Hale explains that it makes sense to use the passive voice when it doesn't matter who is performing the action and when we want the focus of the sentence to be on a subject that is being acted upon.

So it looks like the effectiveness of Palin's and Biden's use of the passive voice in the 2008 Vice Presidential debate is open for debate. In other words, it might have made their points less direct and less vigorous *or* perhaps it served a purpose. So shall we debate it? Or, better yet, let's let Joe Biden and Sarah Palin debate it for old time's sake. And what's that? I get to be the moderator. How exciting! Let's get started.

JB: Good evening. I'm Jenny Baranick. Welcome to the Passive Voice Debate between the former governor of the great state of Alaska Sarah Palin and former senator of the great, well, the state of Delaware Joe Biden. I will provide sentences from their 2008 debate that were constructed in the passive voice by each of the participants, and they will debate about whether or not the passive voice enhances or dilutes their message. Vice President Biden won the thumb war that was to determine who went first . . . .

PALIN: Which must have been luck because he and his capitulator-in -chief usually kowtow and apologize and say, "Thank you, enemy."

BIDEN: With all due respect, Jenny, that's a bunch of malarkey.

JB: Well, this ought to be interesting; let's get started. Vice President Biden, former Governor Palin responded to your suggestion that neither she nor John McCain support adjusting homeowners' principals to keep them from going under by saying the following:

> That is not so, but because that's just a quick answer, I want to talk about, again, my record on energy versus your ticket's energy ticket, also. I think that this is important to come back to, with that energy policy plan again **that was voted for in '05**.

Do you believe her use of the passive voice, as noted in bold, is effective here?

BIDEN: Let me begin by thanking you, Jenny, for hosting this, and it's a pleasure to be with you.

ME (blushing): And it's a pleasure to be with you, Joe.

BIDEN: First, I'd like to start off by noting that former Vice Presidential Nominee Palin devotes as much time talking about energy as I spend at Home Depot—which, you all learned in the first debate, is *a lot* of time. Second, she expresses that the plan "was voted for," but take a walk with me and imagine that this was constructed in the active voice, thusly: "the energy plan that Congress voted for." Stating that "Congress," the subject, performed the verb and "voted" for the energy plan gives the plan more clout because it emphasizes that Congress actively pursued its passing. Stating that the energy plan was simply "voted for" (by whom? Joe Six Pack?) fundamentally undermines the plan's credibility. However, since she most likely disagrees with the plan because it bans drilling in the Arctic, using the passive voice aligns with her purposes.

JB: Ms. Palin, would you like to respond?

PALIN: Let's drill, baby, drill.

JB: Let's move on. Amtrak Joe used passive voice when he was clarifying a comment he made regarding clean coal. He said, "A comment made in a rope line was taken out of context." Do you think he should have used active voice?

PALIN: Darn right I do. The American people have the right to know who took the comment out of context.

BIDEN: Here's the deal. The focus of the sentence is the "comment" and the fact that it was taken out of context. It doesn't matter *who* took it out of context. It wouldn't have mattered if it had been Joe Six Pack, Joey Danco, or any other Joe-adjacent name we used in the 2008 debate. Therefore, using the active voice would have been an abject failure.

JB: Former Presidential Nominee Biden, is the passive voice effective in the following quote from former Reality TV Star Palin: "I do take issue with some of the principles there with that redistribution of wealth principle **that seems to be espoused by you**"?

BIDEN: As I mentioned in a 2012 campaign event, I've known eight presidents, three of them intimately. In other words, I'm experienced.

JB: Is three really considered experienced these days?

BIDEN: And the fact that former Fox News Correspondent Palin used the passive voice here is proof positive that she is subconsciously intimidated by Joe the Biden. If she would have used the active voice and said, "I do take issue with some of the principles there with that redistribution of wealth principle that *you* espoused," she would have really put me on the hook for espousing. But saying that the principles seem to be espoused by me, well, Jenny, it doesn't make her a bad guy, but it does point out that she's not as much of a pit bull as *she* espoused.

PALIN: And for the record, I still think espousing should be between a man and a woman.

JB: Mamma Grizzly, let's move on to Middle Class Joe's use of the passive voice in his quote about education. He said, "The reason **No Child Left Behind was left behind, the money was left behind** ..." Would it have been more effective to express this in the active voice and state who did the leaving behind?

PALIN: Speaking of things left behind, in my own energy-producing state we have billions of barrels of oil and hundreds of trillions of cubic feet of clean, green natural gas left untapped.

JB: You did not answer the question.

PALIN: I may not answer the questions the way that you want to hear, but I'm going to talk straight to the American people.

JB: But aren't you supposed ...

BIDEN: Jenny, can I respond? I could have expressed this sentence in the active voice and said, "The reason George Bush left No Child Left Behind behind was because George Bush left the money behind." But, even for a guy like me who gave a shout out to my "butt buddy" Neil Smith in an Iowa speech, two "behinds" that close together is awkward.

JB: Yes, but not as awkward as calling Neil your butt buddy. Let's move on to sentences about the economy. Caribou Barbie said this in the passive voice: **"Never will we be exploited and taken advantage of again by those who are managing our money and loaning us these dollars."** Uncle Joe?

BIDEN: Starting the sentence with "Never will we be exploited and taken advantage of again" focuses on the victimization of the American people. And while I agree that the American people were victims of the predatory lenders, I would have expressed this sentence in the active voice to focus on the fact that under a Joe Biden and Barack America—I mean, Barack Obama—administration, the financial institutions would never be allowed to prey on the American people again. I'd have said this: "Those who are managing our money and loaning us these dollars will never exploit and take advantage of us again." Actually, I would have said this: "Banks and lenders will never exploit us again." It's more concise.

PALIN: Say it ain't so, Joe. Three sentences in which you discussed the economy were constructed in the passive voice. You said, "No one can deny that the last eight years, we've been dug into a very deep hole here at home with regard to our economy and abroad in terms of our credibility." Who dug us into that hole? You also said, "Corporate America has been rewarded." Who rewarded them, Joe? And you also said that because of Wall Street "the Congress has been put—Democrats and Republicans have been put in a very difficult spot." Who put them in that difficult spot?

BIDEN: Normally, I am known for my excessive passion, but now I am guilty of excessive passive.

JB: We have arrived at the last sentence up for debate. Barracuda said, "John McCain has been the consummate maverick in the Senate over all these years. **He's taken shots left and right from the other party and from within his own party.**" Plugs Biden?

BIDEN: What kind of shots are we talking about here? Tequila shots or Dick Cheney shots? Hahahahaha.

JB: Joe.

BIDEN: Sorry, you all know that my Achilles heel is my lack of discipline. If we expressed this sentence in the active voice, it would be "The other party and his own party have taken shots at him left and right." But that puts the focus on those taking the shots, while I'm sure Palin meant for the emphasis to be on John McCain, and now that the election is over and we won, that's fine by me. As you all know, I really do love John McCain.

JB: Well, that ends tonight's debate. Thank you, Trumpeter Palin and the Bidenator. Neither of you have changed a bit over the years.

PALIN: You betcha!

BIDEN: It's been a pleasure, but, as you all might remember, I would rather be home making love to my wife while my children are asleep.

PALIN: Drill, baby, drill.

JB: Sarah!

Chapter 5

Second Person: Youpergate

As we all know, Sarah Palin belongs to the Republican Party, but she does occasionally cross party lines. For example, when it comes to marijuana, she identifies with the Libertarian platform, claiming that legalizing pot is "no big deal." When it comes to developing Alaska's "God-given resources," she threw her support behind an Independent candidate because she believed he would develop them "responsibly and to the maximum benefit of Alaskans." And when it comes to her scandals, she follows the lead of the Democrats. Like Bill Clinton and former New York Governor Eliot Spitzer, Palin also has a Troopergate.

Bill Clinton's Troopergate involved . . . I'll give you one guess. Yep. Clinton had Arkansas State Troopers arrange sexual liaisons for him and lie to his wife about his whereabouts. Eliot Spitzer's Troopergate scandal actually didn't have anything to do with the $80,000 worth of escort services he procured; he ordered state troopers to keep special records of a political foe, Senate Majority Leader Bruno, in order to undermine him. And the state trooper at the center of Sarah Palin's Troopergate was her brother-in-law, Michael Wooten. She wanted him fired, and the state's public safety commissioner, Walter Monegan, didn't fire him, so Palin fired Walter.

Sarah Palin insisted that she fired Walter for performance related issues but a tape-recorded phone call from her aide Frank Bailey suggested otherwise. Bailey said the following:

Todd and Sarah are scratching their heads, you know. Why on earth hasn't—why is this guy still representing the department? He's a horrible recruiting tool. And, from their perspective, everybody's protecting him. She really likes Walt a lot. But on this issue she feels like it's—she doesn't know why there's absolutely no action for a year on this issue. It's very troubling to her and the family. I can definitely relay that.

On the one hand, Palin admitted that Bailey's call "understandably could be perceived as some kind of pressure, presumably at my direction." But then Philip Gourevitch reports in his *New Yorker* profile on Palin that she told Gourevitch that she couldn't see what the phone call had to do with anything, which she then followed by saying, "It's very disturbing, and it's an issue." So it's an issue, it's not an issue, it's an issue—she changed her mind more than Eliot Spitzer changed prostitutes. But it's this incident that Gourevitch recounted that makes me think Bailey's phone call rattled Sarah: "She began to speak as if Bailey were in the room and she were having it out with him: 'You blundered, Bailey, and you know you did.' She said, 'I'll be talking to him.'"

Imagine you're Gourevitch and you were having a conversation with Palin, and then all of a sudden she broke into a conversation with an imaginary Frank Bailey? I would be thinking, "Can Palin see dead people?"—because, in a sense, Bailey was dead since she totally threw him under the bus. I imagine Palin's sudden shift into second person narrative point of view must have been quite jarring for Gourevitch.

There are three narrative points of view: first, second, and third person. First person point of view is when we use "I" or "we." Palin used it above when she said, "We just found out about it a couple of days ago" and "I'll be talking to him." Second person is when we use "you," which Palin used when she said, "You blundered, Bailey, and you know you did." And third person is when we use "he," "she," "it," "they," or any noun. And Palin used that above when she said, "And yeah, it's very disturbing, and it's an issue." Most likely, your English teacher told you to avoid writing in first and second person. And although third person is generally the accepted narrative point of view for academic writing because it tends to be more objective, I don't believe in firing first or second person from a job unless the reasons really are performance-related. In other words, if you believe using first or second person will enhance your work, discuss your idea with your instructor.

But, like I'm sure Sarah Palin still practices some of the lessons she gleaned from the four colleges she attended, many of us believe we're supposed to avoid writing in first and second person for the rest of our lives. Of course, this is not the case. And if you don't believe me, US leaders have communicated in all three narrative voices:

First person:

"I think that gay marriage should be between a man and a woman."
—*California Gov. Arnold Schwarzengger*

"I did not have sexual relations with that woman."—*President Bill Clinton*

"We know there are known knowns: there are things we know we know. We also know there are known unknowns: that is to say we know there are things we know we don't know. But there are also unknown unknowns—the ones we don't know we don't know."
—*Defense Secretary Donald Rumsfeld, Defense Department*

Second person:

"You all look like happy campers to me. Happy campers you are, happy campers you have been, and, as far as I am concerned, happy campers you will always be."—*Vice President Dan Quayle*

"If you don't mind smelling like peanut butter for two or three days, peanut butter is darn good shaving cream." —*Senator Barry Goldwater*

"If you want a friend in Washington, get a dog."—*President Harry S. Truman*

Third person:

"Too many good docs are getting out of the business. Too many OB-GYNs aren't able to practice their love with women all across this country."—*President George W. Bush*

"A zebra does not change its spots."—*Vice President Al Gore*

"When the President does it, that means it's not illegal."—*President Richard Nixon*

And there you have it: if US leaders communicate in all three narrative points of view, it must be legal.

Out of the three narrative points of view, second person is definitely the most scandalized. It's been accused of being too informal, causing confusion, and being too imprecise. And although I believe that second person can be effective, I do admit that it can be more troublesome than the others narrative points of view precisely because of what happened during Gourevitch's conversation with Palin. Like Sarah, many of us tend to abruptly shift into second person, which can be jarring for our readers. But not only can it be jarring; it can be imprecise, because when we use "you," we are talking directly to our readers, and sometimes when we use "you" we shouldn't be talking directly to our readers—like Sarah does in the following excerpts from *Going Rogue:*

Because Todd had been exposed to conditions in rural Alaska many of us cannot imagine, he'd made tough decisions on his own from a young age. Because of that, principles like honesty, justice and accountability became crucial to his life perspective, and he understood intuitively that **you** get to *choose* how to respond to circumstances around **you**—even those out of **your** control. **You** get to decide what's really important and what **your** attitude will be.

I don't know whether to feel flattered or violated by Todd's intuition. On the one hand, it's flattering that his intuition, which I've never even met, cares enough about me to reveal to Todd that *I* get to choose how to respond to circumstances around *me* and decide what's really important and what *my* attitude will be. But on the other hand, I kind of wish Todd and his intuition would butt out of my life. I like to let the Magic 8 Ball decide how I am going to respond to circumstances around me. I wish Palin would have kept this in the third person like this:

> Because of that, principles like honesty, justice and accountability became crucial to his life perspective, and he understood intuitively that he gets to *choose* how to respond to circumstances around him—even those out of his control. He gets to decide what's really important and what his attitude will be.

Isn't that better? Signs point to yes.

In the following excerpt, she shifted from first to second person:

> On one return trip from Glennallen, we stopped late at night in the middle of nowhere to drop off a campaign sign. Todd had spotted the unmarked dirt road we needed to take, and we rumbled down a narrow lane lined by tall, spindly black spruce until we came to a tiny wooden cabin hidden in the woods. The elderly couple who lived there had called in to a political radio show and voiced their support, so we'd looked them up and promised to deliver them a yard sign, even though **you** wouldn't be able to view it from the main highway.

I don't see how *my* ability to see the yard sign from the main highway is relevant here because, believe it or not, I sat out the Glennallen trip. It would have been more effective if she had written it like this:

> The elderly couple who lived there had called in to a political radio show and voiced their support, so we'd looked them up and promised to deliver them a yard sign, even though it would be impossible to see from the main highway.

Or maybe Sarah knows that I have 20/20 vision, and she was making the point that if Jenny wouldn't be able to see the yard sign from the main highway, then no one would.

And in this excerpt, she seems to call my driving skills into question:

> When the kids and I moved to Juneau in January 2007, Todd and I worked more than 1,300 miles apart. To put that into perspective, it would have been closer for one of us to work in Houston and the other in Minneapolis. Adding to the challenge, **you** can't drive between Prudhoe Bay and our capital city, of course, even if you were up for a four-day road trip. In fact, no one can drive to Juneau.

Well, that's a relief. I thought Sarah saying that I can't drive between Prudhoe Bay and Juneau had something to do with how she felt about my driving skills specifically. But if no one can do it, well, why didn't she just write, "Adding to the challenge, it's impossible to drive between Prudhoe Bay and Juneau."

There are several more:

> Lena is a rough frontier woman. How many American women do **you** know who can weave a grass basket; sew squirrel skins into a garment and adorn it with intricate beadwork; haul a thousand salmon out of the ocean, get them to market in a sailboat, then take some home, fillet them, and serve them for dinner?

Three.

The spirit of the medical team at Landstuhl will change your life if **you** ever experience it.

Great! Landstuhl is on my bucket list. I hope I get sick while I'm there.

As a state chief executive sitting across the table from well-heeled, lawyered-up oil executives, it was a given: **you** have to be committed to the position that is right for the people who hired **you**. **You** can't blink. And we didn't.

I'm not quite sure how my commitment to my job has anything to do with Sarah and the oil executives with their fabulous heels. And I don't know what you're talking about, Sarah; I can totally blink. I'm doing it right now.

Our first day there was a whirlwind. Campaign staff whisked me from the airport to the downtown Hilton and up to an enormous hotel suite with two bedrooms, one for the girls and one for Todd, Trig and me. Track would be there soon, so he and his cousins would stay down the hall. In the center of the room, when **you** first walked in, stood a huge dining/conference table.

Was I was there too? I don't remember. Well, it *was* a whirlwind.

Okay, I don't want you to think that I suffer from narcissistic personality disorder or anything. I know that Palin wasn't specifically talking to or about me in her autobiography. She was using "you" to refer to people in general, but for the most part, she wasn't talking to or about people in general; she was talking about herself and her family. Therefore, maintaining the first or third person narrative voice would have been more accurate and more harmonious. But, having said that, Sarah Palin often employs second person to do the job it really excels at: creating a connection with the audience. For example, in her Republican National Convention speech, she said the following:

> To the families of special-needs . . . To the families of special-needs children all across this country, I have a message for you: for years, you've sought to make America a more welcoming place for your sons and daughters. And I pledge to you that, if we're elected, you will have a friend and advocate in the White House.

Now, imagine she chose to express it in third person:

> For years, families of special-needs children have sought to make America a more welcoming place for their sons and daughters. And I pledge that if we're elected, they will have a friend and advocate in the White House.

By speaking directly to instead of about the families of special-needs children, Palin clearly creates a stronger, more emotional connection. Speaking directly to them also makes her pledge seem more genuine.

In the next excerpt from her RNC speech, Palin uses second person to show her audience that she can identify with their economic struggles:

> Or maybe you are trying to keep your job at a plant in Michigan or in Ohio . . . or you're trying . . . you're trying to create jobs from clean coal, from Pennsylvania or West Virginia. You're trying to keep a small farm in the family right here in Minnesota. How are you—how are you going to be better off if our opponent adds a massive tax burden to the American economy?

She also directly asks her audience a question, which is effective because it forces them to answer, probably even subconsciously, how a massive tax burden is going to make them better off. Had she asked this question a couple of years in the future, after she had fully honed her pit bull wearing lipstick persona, she still would have used the second person, but she would have worded it like this: "And how do ya think that massive tax burden is gonna work out for ya?"

Second person narrative point of view is like taxpayers' money. Like taxpayers' money can be used to achieve good, like as an investment in education, "you" can be used to invest in a meaningful connection with the audience. And like taxpayers' money can be used unfavorably, such as using 1.9 million dollars of it to deal with an Alaskan governor's ethics violations, the use of "you" can unsettle and mislead. So just make sure you use "you" judiciously. You don't want to get yourself caught up in a Youpergate scandal.

Chapter 6

Conciseness: Too Big to Succeed

I n 2009, rumors began to swirl about an impending divorce between Sarah and Todd Palin. There was talk of alleged affairs, naked ring fingers, and properties purchased in Montana. However, in her autobiography, Sarah scoffed at the rumors. She recalls watching Todd "tanned and shirtless" and thinking to herself "Divorce Todd? Have you seen Todd?"

But lest you think that Sarah is that superficial, it wasn't just Todd's good looks that attracted her. She also really liked his 1972 Ford Mustang, in which, she claims, he "roared into [her] life." She also appreciated his independent spirit. And she liked that he didn't "feel the need to fill up the air around [him] with words all the time."

So the old adage is true: opposites attract.

Sarah loves to fill up the air around her with words. In fact, she loves it so much that on the night she and John McCain lost the election, she planned to deliver a concession speech even though vice presidents don't typically deliver concession speeches. She was stymied by McCain's senior staffers, which she said felt like a "slap in the face." And this leads me to a theory: perhaps what has been repeatedly referred to by the media as

Sarah's "rambling," her "incoherent babbling," her "word salads" isn't unintentional. Maybe she's cramming in extra words to make up for the words she wasn't allowed to utter.

Let's have a look at one of those word salads. Actually, this bout of Palin's incoherent babbling was dubbed a different name. In her interview with Charlie Gibson, her response to his question about whether or not the US has the right to cross the Pakistani border without the Pakistani government's consent was so convoluted that Gibson claimed that he got caught in a "blizzard of words." Bundle up! It's about to get blustery:

> In order to stop Islamic extremists, those terrorists who would seek to destroy America and our allies, we must do whatever it takes and we must not blink, Charlie, in making those tough decisions of where we go and even who we target. And let me get back to what's going on there in Pakistan right now. A target needs to be Osama Bin Laden. We cannot give up our fight to find him and John McCain is committed to find him. Remember, John McCain, he said he's going to chase him to the gates of hell, if that's what it takes, to find Osama Bin Laden and to get rid of Osama Bin Laden. We know that he's in that FATA area, the Pakistan mountains, in between Afghanistan and Pakistan. We have got to make sure that we're doing all that we can to get rid of that threat, also.

Brrrrr! There are a couple of lessons we can glean from this blizzard. The most obvious is that before accepting the nomination for vice president of the United States of America one should brush up on one's foreign policy. Another important lesson is that more words aren't necessarily better.

In high school and college, most of us were assigned essays with a required page count. Therefore, we equated longer essays with more sophisticated essays. And we'd freak out about how we were going to amass enough words to fulfill the ten-page requirement, so we'd start adding unnecessary words. "If" became "if it happened to occur that" and "although" became "despite the fact that." We'd take, for example, a nineteen-word sentence like, "Remember, John McCain said he's going to chase Osama Bin Laden to the gates of hell to eliminate him" and expand it to the thirty-three word sentence, "Remember, John McCain, he said he's going to chase him to the gates of hell, if that's what it takes, to find Osama Bin Laden and to get rid of Osama Bin Laden." And we'd be so proud of ourselves because we thought all of those words would impress our teacher.

Well, it turns out that this practice just created a bad habit; in the "real world" conciseness is preferred over verbosity. To see why, let's compare excerpts from two of Sarah Palin's speeches: her 2008 Republican National Convention speech and her infamous 2016 Trump endorsement:

	RNC Speech	Trump Speech
Berating Barack Obama for trying to help his community.	I guess a small-town mayor is kind of like a community organizer, except that you have actual responsibilities.	And he, who would negotiate deals, kind of with the skills of a community organizer maybe organizing a neighborhood tea.
Her tenuous relationship with the media.	But here's a little news flash for all those reporters and commentators: I'm not going to Washington to seek their good opinion. I'm going to Washington to serve the people of this country.	When asked why I would jump into a primary — kind of stirring it up a little bit maybe — and choose one over some friends who are running and I've endorsed a couple others in their races before they decided to run for president, I was told left and right, 'you are going to get so clobbered in the press. You are just going to get beat up and chewed up and spit out.'

Her candidate's wonderful traits.

To the most powerful office on Earth, he would bring the compassion that comes from having once been powerless . . . the wisdom that comes even to the captives, by the grace of God . . . the special confidence of those who have seen evil, and seen how evil is overcome. A fellow prisoner of war, a man named Tom Moe of Lancaster, Ohio, recalls looking through a pinhole in his cell door as Lt. Cmdr. John McCain was led down the hallway, by the guards, day after day. As the story is told, "When John McCain shuffled back from torturous interrogations, he would turn toward Moe's door and flash a grin and thumbs up"—as if to say, "We're going to pull through this." My fellow Americans, that is the kind of man America needs to see us through the next four years.

But, it's amazing, he is not elitist at all. Oh, I just hope you all get to know him more and more as a person and a family man. What he's been able to accomplish, with his, um, it's kind of this quiet generosity. Yeah, maybe his largess, kind of, I don't know, some would say gets in the way of that quiet generosity, and, uh, well, his compassion, but if you know him as a person and you'll get to know him more and more, you'll have even more respect. Not just for his record of success, and the good intentions for America, but who he is as a person. He's not an elitist. And yes, as a multi-billionaire, we still root him on because he roots us on.

If the Trump endorsement speech is a word salad, the RNC speech is like a perfectly layered club sandwich cut into triangles with the crusts removed. Palin's RNC speech is clearly more concise than her Trump endorsement speech, but, as you can see by the comparison of the excerpts, that doesn't necessarily mean she uses fewer words. It means she uses better words and unnecessary words have been edited out. The Trump endorsement speech includes unnecessary phrases like "kind of with the skills of," "kind of stirring it up a little bit maybe," "kind of, I don't know," which make the speech, I don't know, maybe sound kind of sloppy, lazy, and flimsy. The RNC speech, on the other hand, includes strong, vigorous statements, such as "But here's a little news flash for all those reporters and commentators: I'm not going to Washington to seek their good opinion. I'm going to Washington to serve the people of this country." Bam!

Maybe you're thinking that we could edit out the "little" that comes before "news flash," and the sentence would still make sense, or we could change "people of this country" to "this country's people" and save a word, but those changes would weaken the statement. When she says, "people of this country," the emphasis is on the people, which is where she wants it to be. And including the "little" before "newsflash" adds a little bite. And remember, we're dealing with a pit bull here; her style requires a little bite. We never want to edit our words that sacrifice meaning or style. We only want to edit out the words that serve no purpose and, consequently, weigh down our sentences, making our messages weaker and less clear.

For example, we have a tendency to unnecessarily double up on synonyms. In 2010, Sarah Palin came up with a clever way to avoid having to choose between two fabulous words that mean the same thing: she combined those two words to create another word with the same meaning. Specifically, she combined "refute" and "repudiate" and created the word "refudiate." But I guess the following sentences came before she discovered that trick:

He endured such **ridicule** and **mocking** for his vision for Alaska.

I chose to work very hard on a path for **fruitfulness** and **productivity**.

I have given my reasons **candidly** and **truthfully**.

That is desiring government to be **on our side** and **not against us**.

Or she realized that "ridicocking" and "fruitductivity" didn't flow so easily off the tongue. Sorry, Sarah, one of the bolded words in each sentence has got to go.

The unnecessary words Sarah included in the next sentences might be because she is trying to compensate for her Africa gaffe. The McCain staffers revealed that Palin wasn't sure which category Africa fit into, a continent or a country. In these sentences she makes sure she lets us know which category the words fit into.

> Despite his steel core, Todd was shy and quiet **in demeanor**, typical of Yupik men who, unlike some others, don't feel the need to fill up the air around them with words all the time.
>
> We need to put more of an emphasis on **the profession of** teaching.

Sarah, thank you for clarifying, but we already know that shy and quiet are types of demeanors and that teaching is a profession, so feel free to delete the words in bold.

Sarah Palin describes government spending the same way I would describe these sentences: "bloated, overreaching, fat, nauseating." I am going to put them on a diet. Here are the befores and afters:

> Before: But, you know, heaven forbid that we go the opposite direction of a libertarian and what they are believing in.
> After: But, you know, heaven forbid we oppose a libertarian's beliefs.

> Before: We can speak in agreement.
> After: We can agree.

> Before: Now, as for John McCain's adherence to rules and regulations and pushing for even harder and tougher regulations, that is another thing that he is known for though.

After: Now, John McCain is also known for adhering to rules and regulations and pushing for even tougher ones.

Aren't those a little less nauseating?

And the following excerpt from her autobiography contains just one unnecessary word:

> I saw the Alaska Right to Life (RTL) booth, where a poster caught my eye, taking my breath away. It featured the sweetest baby girl swathed in pink, **pretend** angel wings fastened to her soft shoulders. "That's you, baby," I whispered to Piper, as I have every year since she smiled for the picture as an infant.

I am not an angel expert, but I imagine that angels beget angels. In other words, Sarah, you didn't have to tell us that your daughter's angel wings were "pretend" because we know that you are no angel.

Now, let's take on a real challenge and edit an excerpt from her Trump endorsement speech for conciseness. It's almost as bloated as Trump's ego:

> But, it's amazing, he is not elitist at all. Oh, I just hope you all get to know him more and more as a person and a family man. What he's been able to accomplish, with his, um, it's kind of this quiet generosity. Yeah, maybe his largess, kind of, I don't know, some would say gets in the way of that quiet generosity, and, uh, well, his compassion, but if you know him as a person and you'll get to know him more and more, you'll have even more respect. Not just for his record of success, and the good intentions for America, but who he is as a person. He's not an elitist. And yes, as a multi-billionaire, we still root him on because he roots us on.

I have comments:

> But, it's amazing, he is not elitist ~~at all~~. **(If he's not elitist, then he's not elitist at all.)** Oh, I just hope you all get to know him more ~~and~~

~~more~~ (**One more is enough.**) as a person and a family man. What he's been able to accomplish, with his, ~~um, it's kind of this~~ quiet generosity (**very quiet**) Yeah, maybe his *largess* (**"Largess" doesn't mean what she thinks it means. It means "generosity," so the rest of this sentence doesn't make sense. His generosity can't get in the way of his generosity.**), ~~kind of, I don't know,~~ some would say gets in the way of that quiet generosity, and, ~~uh, well,~~ his compassion (**Ha ha ha ha ha!**), but if you know him as a person and you'll get to know him more ~~and more,~~ you'll have even more respect not just for his record of success, and the good intentions for America, but who he is as a person. He's not an elitist (**You already said this**). And yes, as a multi-billionaire, we still root him on because he roots us on.

And here is proof that "yuge" isn't necessarily better:

> But, it's amazing, he is not elitist. Oh, I just hope you all get to know him more as a person and a family man and see what he's been able to accomplish with his quiet generosity and compassion. If you do, you'll have even more respect for his record of success, his good intentions for America, and who he is. Even though he's a multi-billionaire, we still root him on because he roots us on.

The concise version almost makes me want to get to know more about Trump's largess. Almost.

Chapter 7

Clarity:
Splodey Heads

Since 2008, Sarah Palin has threatened to—I mean, flirted with—the idea of running for president. Prior to the 2016 election, Sarah Palin explained on *Good Morning America* that she put the decision in God's hands, and if God opened that door she "was built to run through it." God did what any benevolent being would do and dead bolted that door shut, but I do agree with Sarah that she is built to run through the door. She's an exceptional runner. Her personal best marathon time is faster than both Al Gore's and Paul Ryan's, and even though John Edwards' personal best is faster than hers (3:30 to her 3:59), he was thirty when he ran his; she was forty-one and had given birth to four kids kids. In fact, she is so passionate about running that she and Todd named their first kid Track.

All of the Palin children seem to be named after things their parents have a personal connection to. Their eldest daughter Bristol was named after Bristol Bay, which is where the family likes to fish. Their second eldest daughter was named Willow after an Alaskan town. Piper, their youngest daughter, is thought to be named after the Piper Super Cub, which is an Alaskan bush plane. And their youngest, their son Trig, was named after their connection to math. Just kidding, Trig is Norse for *honesty*. Now, what exactly their connection to honesty is, I don't know.

But let's say you're a parent-to-be and you hate running, you don't fish, and you don't speak Norse, how do you pick a name? Well, you can hire a baby name consultant. There's one in Switzerland that promises to create a rhythmic, unique, meaningful name for your baby, and it will only cost you thirty grand. Or, if you're one of those elitist parents who would rather deposit that thirty thousand dollars in your kids' college fund, you can go to the Palin Family Baby Names Generator website. It's free! I tried it; my kids' names would be Slaw, Hazmat, Tarp, Hamhock, and Amtrak.

Obviously, the website exists to poke fun at the Palins for giving their children such unique names. But it's not like the Palins are the only parents who have done so. Nicholas Cage named his son Kal-El, which is Superman's birth name. Penn Teller named his daughter Moxie Crimefighter. And Jason Lee named his son Pilot Inspektor. Here's the difference, though: I'm pretty sure that Jason Lee wouldn't be surprised to find that others found the name Pilot Inspektor unusual. That is not the case with Sarah Palin. She said, "It took us aback to realize that the name [Track] sounded odd to others."

What this says to me is that Sarah Palin might have some issues with empathy—the ability to relate to the feelings, thoughts, or attitudes of others. If she could relate well to others, it wouldn't have taken her aback that others thought naming her firstborn after a 400-meter oval was odd. And, perhaps, it's this lack of empathy that caused several Alaskans to believe that Sarah suffers from narcissistic personality disorder, which in addition to a lack of empathy includes a pattern of grandiosity and a need for admiration.

Do I believe that Sarah suffers from narcissistic personality disorder? Well, I don't think it's that simple. I believe she suffers from a split personality, only one of which suffers from narcissistic personality disorder. Half the time her words exhibit a lack of empathy, a pattern of grandiosity, and a need for admiration, and half the time they don't. In other words, half the time she doesn't take the time to get into her audience's head, she exaggerates her importance, and she shows off.

An example of when she failed to get into her audience's head is when she used the term "splodey head" in her speech at the Western Conference Summit. She said, "It's really funny to me to see the splodey heads keep 'sploding over this movement," the movement being Donald Trump's GOP nomination and the splodey heads being the heads of the Republicans who doubted the possibility of his nomination. But what columnist Seth Millstein understandably questions in his article on Bustle.com is "What, exactly, makes something 'splodey'"? He wonders if "splodey" means "in an exploding fashion" or if it means that "these Republican heads were already in the process of exploding" or if it means they have heads "with a high propensity to explode."

If Palin didn't also exhibit a pattern of grandiosity and need for admiration, I wouldn't diagnose her use of "splodey head" as a symptom of narcissistic personality disorder; I would diagnose it as a curse: the Curse of Knowledge. Curse of Knowledge is a term coined by linguist Steven Pinker, which he describes as "a difficulty in imagining what it is for someone else not to know what you know." Consequently, he explains, "We're more likely to overestimate the reader's familiarity with our little world than to underestimate it." For example, "splodey" might be a word that Sarah, Todd, Track, Bristol, Willow, Piper, and Trig use all the time, so Sarah didn't even consider that her audience wasn't familiar with it. If she had been more in tune with her audience, she might have used a word that her audience was more likely to be familiar with (e.g., exploding, combustive, ignitable) or she could have provided a quick explanation, like she does when her non-narcissistic personality is present. In *Going Rogue: An American Life*, realizing that those of us from the Lower Forty-Eight might not be familiar with the Alaska-related things she discusses in her book, she provides some helpful explanations, like this one about Alaskan sports:

Libby Riddles, the first woman to win the Iditarod, the famed 1,100-mile sled dog race, had just introduced me as the first woman governor of the state.

Providing an explanation of the Iditarod is helpful. Providing a phonetic spelling would have been really helpful.

And this one about Alaskan celebrities:

> There was more celebration after the speech, as some of our home-grown talent entertained us, including Atz Kilcher, the father of the pop singer Jewel.

Sorry, Atz, but Sarah's right; I would have had no idea who you were if she hadn't mentioned you were Jewel's father. And Sarah even took her explaining a step further and clarified that she was speaking about Jewel, the pop singer, as opposed to the other famous Jewels: Jewel De'Nyle, the porn star; Jewel Joseph Newman, the African-American politician and community organizer from Baton Rouge; Jewel Mische, the Philppine-American actress, or John Jewel, the sixteenth-century Bishop of Salisbury.

And this one about Alaskan fashion:

> The two of them were big golfers and liked to wear visors and golf shorts around a town where a lot of folks wore Carhartts and Bunny Boots, the fat rubber army boots that are incomparable for keeping your feet warm and dry (and the more duct-taped they are, the more Alaskan you are).

Without the Bunny Boot explanation, I would have just assumed they were boots made out of bunnies that Sarah shot from a plane.

And then there were clearly times when her narcissistic personality reared its head while she was writing her autobiography:

> I was already second-guessing my decision to drive the twelve-hour round-trip to the Valdez meet-and-greet campaign event in the middle of winter—a distance like going from Raleigh, North Carolina, to New York City.

This excerpt doesn't lack an explanation; it contains a confusing one. Why did she include the explanation "like going from Raleigh, North Carolina to New York City"? She already explained that the drive was twelve hours round-trip, so what's so special about the drive from Raleigh to New York City? Why not Little Rock to Pensacola? Or San Francisco to Los Angeles? Am I missing something?

And in this excerpt, Palin expects her audience to be able to read her mind and understand that she didn't actually mean what she said:

> In February 2008, Hillary Clinton publicly pointed out some of this media favoritism. Weeks later, I responded to her comments during a *Newsweek* Women and Leadership event in Los Angeles: "I say this with all due respect to Hillary Clinton . . . but when I hear a statement like that coming from a woman candidate, with any kind of perceived whine about the excess criticism . . . I think, man, that doesn't do us any good." I wasn't really accusing her of whining.

I guess it was just a perceived accusation.

•   At times I felt like the mayor of Peyton Place.

I've never heard of Peyton Place, so I looked it up and found out that it's the name of a 1956 novel that remained on the *New York Times* Bestseller list for fifty-nine weeks. Also, the term "Peyton Place" is commonly used to refer to a small town that holds scandalous secrets. (Wasilla, here I come!) So should Palin have provided an explanation of Peyton Place? Probably not. The book was on the bestseller list for fifty-nine weeks. It was also made into a television series. And apparently it's a common allusion. *I've* just never heard of it. As Steven Pinker said, "Every audience is spread out along a bell curve of sophistication, and inevitably we'll bore a few at the top while baffling a few at the bottom." Apparently, I'm one of those baffled ones at the bottom.

And because I was one of those baffled ones at the bottom, I looked up "Peyton Place," but that's only because I'm writing this book. If I weren't writing this book, there's no way I would have taken the time to look it up. Instead, I would have subconsciously decided what it meant—and I would have been wrong. Because I never would have associated Wasilla, the home of the Loose Moose Café, with scandalous secrets, I would have assumed that the "Peyton Place" comparison suggested that Wasilla was a bit provincial. It's like what Dr. Carla O'Dell, CEO of American Product & Quality Center, said, "If you don't give someone information, they'll make up something to fill the void."

The likelihood of baffled reader filling the void with his or her own ideas is why it's also important to provide your readers with specific details instead of vague concepts. We tend to, for example, rely on these vague concepts instead of specific examples in our résumés, cover letters, and proposals. Instead of providing specific examples of our accomplishments, we simply use broad descriptions like "hardworking," "team player," "innovative," "enthusiastic," "passionate," and "committed to excellence"—which actually tell our audience nothing. Actually, they do tell our audience one thing: that we sound just like everyone else. But I know one person who would never shroud her accomplishments in broad, generic phrases: Sarah Louise Palin. When Governor Sarah Louise Palin gave her resignation speech, she didn't hesitate to provide a long list of specific details about her accomplishments as a governor:

- We created a petroleum integrity office to oversee safe development. We held the line FOR Alaskans on Point Thomson—and finally for the first time in decades—they're drilling for oil and gas.
- We have AGIA, the gasline project—a massive bi-partisan victory (the vote was 58 to 1!)—also succeeding as intended—protecting Alaskans as our clean natural gas will flow to energize us, and America, through a competitive, pro-private sector project. This is the largest private sector energy project, ever. THIS is energy independence.
- And ACES—another bipartisan effort—is working as intended and industry is publicly acknowledging its success. Our new oil

and gas "clear and equitable formula" is so Alaskans will no longer be taken advantage of. ACES incentivizes NEW exploration and development and JOBS that were previously not going to happen with a monopolized North Slope oil basin.

- We cleaned up previously accepted unethical actions; we ushered in bi-partisan Ethics Reform.

- We also slowed the rate of government growth, we worked with the Legislature to save billions of dollars for the future, and I made no lobbyist friends with my hundreds of millions of dollars in budget vetoes . . . but living beyond our means today is irresponsible for tomorrow.

- We took government out of the dairy business and put it back into private-sector hands—where it should be.

- We provided unprecedented support for education initiatives, and with the right leadership, finally filled long-vacant public safety positions. We built a sub-Cabinet on Climate Change and took heat from Outside special interests for our biologically-sound wildlife management for abundance.

- We broke ground on the new prison.

- And we made common sense conservative choices to eliminate personal luxuries like the jet, the chef, the junkets . . . the entourage.

- And the Lt. Governor and I said "no" to our pay raises. So much success in this first term—and with this success I am proud to take credit. . . for hiring the right people! Our goal was to achieve a gasline project, more fair oil and gas valuation, and ethics reform in four years. We did it in two. It's because of the people . . . good public servants surrounding the Governor's office, with servants' hearts and astounding work ethic . . . THEY are Alaska's success!

Bam! If I were going to hire a governor and a résumé that listed all these specific accomplishments came across my desk after I had spent all day sifting through ones that said "passionate about approving state budgets" and "works well with legislature," it would be so refreshing. I would seriously consider hiring her—until I got to the part that said "Reason for leaving: too many ethics violations."

Now, Sarah Palin isn't always so forthcoming with specific details—and this, of course, must be when the personality that suffers from narcissistic personality disorder takes over. For example, Sarah Palin's infamous answer to Katie Couric's question about what publications she reads "to stay informed and to understand the world" was incredibly vague: "All of 'em, any of 'em that have been in front of me over all these years." So what do we do when we're not given information? We make something up to fill the void. So from what I know of Sarah Palin, I would have guessed she meant *The Last Frontier, Guns & Ammo, Runner's World*, and *Trump Magazine* (before it folded in 2009 after two years in circulation).

However, if Palin didn't occasionally suffer from narcissistic personality disorder, there are a couple of other reasons her answer might have been so vague. She understands the world not by reading publications but by analyzing moose droppings. (It's a thing.) Or, like many of us, she's so focused on being concise and not bombarding her audience with too much information that she shies away from adding details. But, remember, being concise doesn't mean that we eliminate anything that will enhance our audience's experience, and studies have found that specific details do, in fact, enhance the audience's experience. They increase the audience's interest in the material, their ability to recall the material, and their ability to trust the material. But, of course, we don't want to include details that are irrelevant to our purposes. There has to be a reason we provide the details we do—unlike these specific details Palin used in her autobiography:

> Todd drove me into Anchorage in our Ford Extended Bronco on a sunny but frigid November day.

Todd drove Sarah to Anchorage in their Ford Extended Bronco in 2002 so Sarah could be interviewed by Frank Murkowski about taking over his Senate seat when he assumed the governorship. I am onboard with the specific detail about the weather—"sunny but frigid" could very well symbolize the way Sarah Palin felt about the interview: hopeful but nervous. But the Ford Extended Bronco? Did Ford pay her for product placement?

> Clark Perry, a high-energy, redheaded high school friend who worked for the state's Department of Corrections, came to the house the day I kicked off the campaign.

The only reason I can imagine that she included the color of Clark's hair is because she wanted to make it clear that she's not a gingerphobe. However, if that were the case, I would think she would have worded it like she did when she wanted to make it clear that she wasn't a homophobe because she had a gay friend. And in that case, she would have written, "Clark Perry, a high-energy high school friend, who *happens* to have red hair."

> They [a couple who supported her gubernatorial campaign] treated us to slices of homemade rhubarb pie, then gave us a whole blueberry pie that we shared with friends after our 800-mile, 40-hour round-trip, driven to the sound of the Black Eyed Peas and an old L.L. Cool J remix we found in the glove box.

In the war over cake versus pie, I am a pie person, so it delighted me that Sarah provided us with a little pie porn. Rhubarb, yum! Blueberry, yes! Also, showing that the couple produced two different kinds of pies pays homage to their pie versatility. But why did she feel that it was important to let her readers know that she and Todd saved the pies until they got home and then proceeded to share them with friends? To exhibit their restraint? Their generosity? And then, of course, she provided specific details about the music they listened to, and I'm not sure envisioning Sarah and Todd kickin' it old school and jammin' to "I'm gonna knock you out. Mama said knock you out" really enhances my reading experience.

But as much as we don't want to incorporate unnecessary details, having graded and critiqued thousands of essays, reports, and cover letters, I promise you that we tend to provide too few specific details rather than too many. And, oftentimes, even when we think we're being specific, we're not. For example, after Palin answered Couric's question about the publications that she read, Couric provided Palin with the opportunity to be more specific and asked, "Can you name a few?" Palin answered, "I have a vast variety of sources where we get our news too. Alaska isn't a foreign country, where, it's kind of suggested and it seems like, 'Wow, how could you keep in touch with what the rest of Washington, D.C. may be thinking and doing when you live up there in Alaska?" She did what many of us do when asked to be more specific: she expanded on her answer, but she didn't get more specific. Sarah needed to take her own advice and drill, baby, drill until she got to something concrete. Similarly, in these excerpts from her Trump speech, she starts out with something vague and then gets a little bit more specific, but she doesn't drill far enough:

> Where, in the private sector, you actually have to balance budgets in order to prioritize — to keep the main thing, the main thing — and he knows the main thing. A president is to keep us safe economically and militarily.

Palin begins by telling us that Donald Trump is going to keep "the main thing," and you can't really get more vague than referring to something as "the main thing." But she does get a little bit more specific by letting us know that "the main thing" actually refers to two main things: economic safety and military safety. As far as economic safety, Donald Trump managed to become a billionaire, so I am not as *invested* in hearing specific examples about how he will ensure our economic safety as I am about how he will ensure our military safety. And I am especially interested in his military strategy because his approach of alienating himself from US allies seems a bit unorthodox.

But Palin doesn't get specific, so let's see what Trump, himself, has to say about his military strategy. In an interview on *Meet the Press* Chuck Todd asked Trump, "Who do you talk to for military advice right now?" Trump must have been inspired by Palin's performance in her Katie Couric interview because he answered, "Well, I watch the shows. I mean, I really see a lot of great — you know, when you watch your show, and all of the other shows, and you have the generals, and you have certain people that you like." Trump did manage to get a little bit more specific after Todd asked him if he had a go-to. "Probably there are two or three," he said. So we're getting somewhere. We went from "all of the other shows" to "two or three." And, then—eureka! Trump finally struck a specific detail. He said, "I mean, I like Bolton. I think he's, you know, a tough cookie, knows what he's talking about."

Unfortunately, he was referring to Ambassador John Bolton, not Michael Bolton. But hear me out, Trump. Michael Bolton was described in the *Independent* as "a purveyor of melodramatic power ballads that bash you into submission with their terrifying choruses and sanctimonious lyrics." Sounds like a powerful military strategy to me!

> But, it's amazing; he [Trump] is not elitist at all. Oh, I just hope you all get to know him more and more as a person and a family man.

Again, Palin starts out with a broad concept: Trump is not elitist. And, as before, she gets a little more specific: more specifically, he is not elitist because he is a person and a family man. I don't quite know what kind of specific example she could provide that would help prove he is a person. A copy of his birth certificate, perhaps? But she could definitely include some specific details that prove he's a family man. For example, she could have provided this heartwarming quote Trump said about his daughter: "I've said if Ivanka weren't my daughter, perhaps I'd be dating her."

Now, let's move on to the second symptom of Sarah Palin's narcissistic personality disorder, her pattern of grandiosity. In other words, half the time, she has an exaggerated idea of her importance. And, as you know, when we have an exaggerated idea of our importance, we think everything we think and do is worth relating. For example, in Palin's autobiography, she spends over half a page recounting this childhood memory:

One of these wooden sidewalks was the scene of one of my earliest memories: my attempt to fly. I couldn't have been more than four years old and was walking to my friend's house all by myself because in such a small town, little kids gained their independence early. My friend and I were supposed to go to catechism together, and I was anxious to get to her big, busy, Catholic family, which bustled with a dozen brothers and sisters. I kept to the wooden planks that paralleled the town's main dirt road, and as the warm boards echoed under my feet, I got to thinking: I had seen eagles and dragonflies, and ptarmigan fly, but I had never seen a person fly. That didn't make any sense to me. Hadn't anyone ever tried it before? Why couldn't someone just propel herself up into the air and get it done?

I stopped and looked up at the summer sky, then down at the dirt road below. Then I simply jumped. I didn't care who might see me. I wanted to fly more than I worried about what I looked like. My knees took most of the impact, and I scraped them both.

Well, that didn't work, I thought. So I got up, dusted myself off, and kept walking.

So, let me get this straight: a four-year old Sarah Palin wanted to fly, so she jumped— not off of something high like a house or an igloo—she jumped off the ground. Then, she fell. And then she got up and continued walking. Only in Alaska!

In addition to manifesting as the belief that every detail of our lives is riveting, a pattern of grandiosity can also manifest as the belief that our way is superior. For example, in her autobiography, Palin describes a *Vogue* interview she did while she was governor:

Since fashion trends weren't my top interest, I kept bringing the *Vogue* writer's questions back to national security and energy independence. That made it tough for her as she was doing her best to write for readers who cared about the latest Fifth Avenue styles and probably wouldn't be caught dead in a pair of Sorels. She finally had to stop me and nicely say she'd heard enough about energy. I just couldn't pivot from hydropower to high fashion, so the interview wasn't that great for the readers, I'm sure.

Here's an idea for you, Sarah: if you know that your interview is not going to be great for the readers, don't give the interview. I know that sounds harsh, and I do get where Sarah is coming from. She wants us to know that she's into important stuff like hydropower, not superficial stuff like fashion. She must have not wanted to return her $150,000 wardrobe purchased by the McCain staff because she wanted to recycle it and turn it into power. And, of course, I agree that national security and energy independence are more important than Chanel and Jimmy Choos (okay, maybe not more important than Jimmy Choos), but the fact is that Palin knew that the readers wouldn't appreciate what she had to say. In other words, it wasn't like she was discussing hydropower in hopes of enlightening her readers about an issue she thought would matter to them; she was simply discussing it because she wanted to. It was all about her needs.

Now, we know that the other half of the time she isn't so narcissistic. And this is evident by that way she communicated when she worked in the energy industry. In *Going Rogue,* she explained her method of communicating:

> You have to send messages independently to each group: To explorers, you have to speak of expansion and access to get their new discoveries to market. To producers, you speak of inducements such as a stable investment climate. To pipeline owners, you speak of open seasons and shipping and tariff rates that let them recover costs. Most important, to the resource owners—in this case, the people of Alaska—you speak of getting the oil safely out of the ground into our cars and homes and businesses to provide economic and security benefits.

In other words, she actually took the needs of her audience into consideration and communicated to them only that which concerned them. She didn't write one giant message that included information that concerned all the groups, expecting each group to take the time to parse through it themselves and figure out what was applicable to them. It was all about their needs.

And that, my friends, takes us to the last symptom of Palin's narcissistic personality disorder: the need for admiration. And narcissistic personality disorder aside, I can see why Palin exhibited this need for admiration. According to the 2009 Gallup Poll, the perceived whiner, Hillary Clinton, edged out Palin as America's most admired woman. So in her 2009 autobiography, Palin may have been a little desperate to impress her readers, and, therefore, she uncharacteristically used some fancy words. Doing anything fancy is uncharacteristic for Sarah because if you know Sarah you know that she hates anything that is elite: the media elite, the liberal elite, the Republican elite, the caviar-eating elite. Yes, she once had a job scraping the eggs out of fish bellies and "thought it was hilarious that the company would slap a caviar label on the . . . er, delicacy . . . and sell it to elite consumers for loads of money." But in her desperation to impress, she used a few of those elite words in *Going Rogue*.

Many of you might be thinking that there's nothing desperate about using fancy words, that a sophisticated vocabulary reflects intelligence. And, of course, you can use the fanciest of words in your writing. If you're sure that everyone in your audience knows what "cupidity" means, then by all means, use it. But if you're not sure, just use its synonym "greed" because you know the ones who are not familiar with it are going to think "cupidity" has something to do with a famous little cherub and they're not going to look it up. If you're sure that everyone in your audience knows the meaning of the word "pluvious," go for it, but if not, just use the word "rainy." And if that's the case, you should really ask yourself why you are hanging out with people who know what "pluvious" means. But the point is that we don't write to impress our readers; we write to communicate clearly to them. As Steven Pinker says, "[Good writing] makes the reader feel like a genius. Bad writing makes the reader feel like a dunce."

Well, I felt like a dunce when I read the following sentence from Palin's book:

Halcro was a wealthy, effete young chap who had taken over his father's local Avis Rent A Car.

Okay, I admit it: I didn't know what "effete" meant, so I had to look it up. And, as you know, if I weren't writing this book, I wouldn't have taken the time to do so, and I would have just made up my own definition. And my definition would have been "effeminate." But I would have been wrong. "Effete" has a few meanings: lacking in wholesome vigor, worn-out, or sterile. Now, in order to figure out which one of those she meant, I have to research to see if Halcro has any kids.

I *am* familiar with the elite word that Sarah used in the following excerpt:

This mélange of views served as a constant reminder of my mission in office to develop our state's resources in the best interest of the environment and of the people—including getting a gasline built.

But tell me, honestly, have you ever used the word "mélange" in a sentence? And if you have, could the person on the receiving end of the word "mélange" refrain from rolling his or her eyes? Sarah, I know you. You revel in your folksiness. Tell me you weren't just dying to use the word "hodge-podge."

Of course, Sarah Palin isn't the only author suspected of suffering from narcissism. A biography of Nathaniel Hawthorne portrays him as having a "powerful narcissistic craving for fame and immortality." But, like Sarah Palin, I think Nathaniel Hawthorne only suffers from narcissism half the time. A quote attributed to Hawthorne, "Easy reading is damn hard writing," illustrates that he understood that good writers must carefully customize their explanations, details, content, and language for their audience—so, you know, their heads don't splode.

Chapter 8

Clichés: A Barrel of Naughty Monkeys

Shortly before catapulting Sarah Palin into the political spotlight, McCain catapulted another attractive, charismatic, terribly under-qualified woman into the political spotlight: Paris Hilton. One of McCain's campaign ads claimed that Obama was nothing more than a mega-celebrity of the Paris Hilton ilk. I'm pretty sure that the comparison between Obama and Hilton was meant to suggest that Obama wasn't qualified to run the country, but Paris Hilton thought it meant that she *was* qualified to run the country and launched a campaign ad of her own. Tanning poolside in a bikini, Paris assured us that she was "like totally ready to lead." She also hinted that Rihanna would most likely be her VP pick. Sure, a Paris/Rihanna presidency would be hotly contested, but it would finally enable the US to join our neighbors, Canada and Mexico, under the umbrella (ella ella ella) of hot world leaders.

Ironically, though, Sarah and Paris have a lot more in common than Barack and Paris. Sarah and Paris both have catchphrases. They are both reality TV stars. They both have *New York Times* bestselling autobiographies. They both shop at Saks Fifth Avenue. They even wear the same shoes. Paris Hilton totally owns a pair of the Naughty Monkey heels that Sarah Palin famously wore when she gave her 2008 RNC speech.

When Palin catapulted those Red Naughty Monkey Double Dare heels into the political spotlight, they began flying off the shelves. (Not literally, of course. They're Naughty Monkeys, not flying monkeys.) So did her rimless glasses. Wig makers were even flooded with requests for the Palin updo. And the public didn't just clamber to appropriate Palin's 2008 look. In 2010, they also clambered to appropriate a question she used in her speech to the first Tea Party convention: "How's that hopey-changey stuff working out for ya?" The *New York Times* article "'Hopey-Changey' Alive" documented the numerous ways others adapted her saying:

- **"How's that working out for ya?"** — *Herman Cain*
- **"Someone really should borrow Sarah Palin's question and ask [Prime Minister] David Cameron: 'How's that hopey-changey thing working out for ya?'"** — *The Observer*, London
- **"Hey, seniors, how's that no-tax thing been working out for ya?"** — *Letter to the editor, The Philadelphia Inquirer*
- **"How's that freedom-loving movement working out for ya, Egypt? Don't ask Obama (who tossed Mubarak to the curb with both hands) — he's busy invading Libya."** — *Atlas Shrugs* blog
- **"Hey Hezbollah, how's running Lebanon working out for ya? Yea, not easy anymore when you're in charge is it"** — *Surfview Capital* via Twitter
- **"If you think schlepping a tripod along with your D.S.L.R. isn't worth it because you're convinced you can get a clean shot if you just concentrate hard enough, we have to ask . . . how's that working out for ya?"** — *Engadget* blog
- **"How's that working out for ya, B.C.?"** — *The Province*, Vancouver, British Columbia
- **"How's that Randy Pauly thing working out for ya?"** — Commenter on the *Daily Dish* blog

- **"So how's that distaste with the Hollywood liberal elite thing working out for ya, Mama Bear?"** — *The Las Vegas Review-Journal*

- "So how's that 'American Idol' thing working out for ya, Lee DeWyze?" — *Fresnobeehive* blog
- "How's that property-tax reduction that Gov. Rendell promised working out for ya?" — *The Intelligencer Journal/New Era*, Lancaster, PA
- "Incidentally, how's all that big smiley, TelePrompTery, cardboard Greek-Temply, beer-summity hope and change working out for ya?" — *The Arkansas Democrat-Gazette*
- How's that not name-y because it invalidates your argument thingy working out for ya?" — *Tina Dupuy*, syndicated columnist
- "Hey Sarah, how's that cross-hairsy, targety thing working out for ya now?" — Question in a "State of the Union drinking game" on About.com that, if President Obama had actually posed it in his address, would have obliged players to down a six-pack.
- "Hey, everybody, how's that code of silence working out for ya?" — *The Chicago Sun-Times*

And that, my friends, is how clichés become clichés. A cliché is an expression that was once original, clever, and evocative but has become tedious and lifeless through overuse. Or as Paris Hilton would say, "It's not hot." Palin's question "How's that Hopey-Changey stuff working out for you?" likely resonated so strongly because the hope that Obama had heralded two years earlier was quickly disintegrating as the change he had promised was not materializing. Federal wages were being frozen, unemployment was still rampant, there seemed to be no end in sight for the war in Afghanistan. So by trivializing "hope" and "change" by slapping Y's on the end of them and delivering the question with her signature snark, Palin tapped right into the public's frustration and anger. She struck a chord and it spread like wildfire until everyone and their mother couldn't seem to conceive of a better way to express their disdain. So they appropriated hers.

But let me ask you something? When I wrote that her words "struck a chord," did you feel the vibration of the notes deep in your heart? When I wrote that her words "spread like wildfire," did you feel the hot whoosh of the orange flames as you watched them furiously engulf everything in their path? When I wrote that "everyone and their mother" started using her expression did you chuckle because "and their mother" is a clever little addition to emphasize the quantity? You probably didn't even notice, did you? Or maybe you even rolled your eyes because you'd heard those sayings so many times. So maybe the first couple of times columnists adapted Palin's phrase, it was clever, but after everyone and their mother started doing it, it was like been there, done that.

In addition to making your writing as lifeless as the turkeys being decapitated behind Palin on the day she pardoned one of the lucky ones, clichés often just waste space. For example, in *Going Rogue* she wrote, "The Palin-Kallstrom family was also the most generous I have ever met, willing to give the shirts off their backs." But there's actually no point in including the cliché "willing to give the shirts off their backs" to describe her husband's family because it simply reiterates a point that she already made: that they're generous. It doesn't illuminate anything. What would have been illuminating is if she replaced the cliché with some specific examples of generous things the Palin-Kallstrom family had done. For example, perhaps they made moose stew for the entire neighborhood every Sunday evening. Maybe Todd's dad gave Sarah his prized rifle when he heard that she was flying to Arizona to meet John McCain—just in case she saw a wolf on her way. Maybe Todd's half-sister gave Sarah some of the booty from the house she allegedly burgled. What *isn't* generous is Sarah Palin's use of empty clichés rather than specific examples because specifics are more interesting and informative to readers.

But, of course, "willing to give the shirts off their backs" isn't the only cliché Palin used in her autobiography. You know Sarah; she's "in it to win it." Here's the whole kit and caboodle:

I spoke off the cuff
The smoke cleared
Let the chips fall where they may
Small potatoes
Be-all and end-all
Money-where-your-mouth-is

Let's get this show on the road
Stir the pot
Bring home the bacon
Fire in my belly
Bridles your passion
Politicians bending with the wind
Hit the hay
Knocked them out of the park
Music to my ears
My face fell
Ran the gamut
I was no spring chicken
The world was their oyster
But she dug in her heels
Sometimes life throws you a curve ball
We put our foot down
He pulled himself up by his bootstraps
Too big for my britches

Now, what do all these clichés have in common? Let me give you a hint: Do you think that Sarah really had a fire in her belly? I've never had moose stew, but I doubt that actual combustion is a side effect. Do you think her face actually fell off? I heard that the campaign spent thousands on her makeup, but it couldn't have been that heavy, right? What these clichés have in common is that they are metaphors—and metaphors are awesome—which is why these clichés probably became so popular in the first place. Metaphors are so awesome because they delight us by comparing things or ideas that we normally wouldn't associate.

So instead of relying on a stale, used up cliché, why not create your own original metaphor to describe the situation? I'll tell you why. It's hard. Sarah Palin expresses this difficulty when she described her experience at a Florida rally. She writes, "At go time, he opened the door, and another tidal wave of sound rushed in. I looked out at the sea of people, so large and stunning that I have nothing to compare it to." First of all, she's lying. She did have something to compare it to because she compared it to a "sea of people," which is a cliché. It would have been more accurate if she had said that she had nothing original to compare it to. But she also lied because a few lines down she does find a comparison. She writes, "But the only time I'd ever seen a crowd this large, even as a spectator, was at a Broncos-Seahawks game in Seattle twenty years before." Now, I know that comparing the size of the crowd at her rally to the size of the crowd at a football game isn't a metaphor, but it is a helpful comparison because it's an image most of us can relate to. Even if we've never been to CenturyLink Field, or any other football stadium, in person, we've seen one on TV. Therefore, the comparison enables us to actually envision the magnitude of the crowd.

But Palin doesn't always struggle to create metaphors. She actually has some pretty great ones in her autobiography: She describes the Alaskan state legislature as place "where the trading of favors seemed to run through the ventilation system as a substitute for air."

Palin could have relied on a tired cliché here and wrote something like "the trading of favors filled the air," but by using a metaphor that compares the trading of favors to air running through the ventilation system, she says so much more. She says that not only do the favors fill the air, they are transported invisibly from office to office. The invisibility of these favors emphasizes the sneakiness of this corrupt practice because no one ever knows who is trading favors with whom.

Or maybe my cynicism caused me to misinterpret "favors." Maybe the state legislators are very nice people and the ventilation system is circulating with offers to pick up dry cleaning and buy lunch.

She describes her encounter with McCain's Secret Service men as follows: "A small knot of men whisked us into a tinted-window Suburban."

Comparing the Secret Service men to a knot enables the reader to visualize the Palins' experience. We see men in black suits huddled so closely that they're seemingly interwoven. Comparing the Secret Service men to a "knot" is also clever because the purpose of knots, like the Secret Service, is to keep things safe and secure.

If you'll indulge me, I'd like to take my two favorite metaphors about men and combine them into a super metaphor: "It's raining knots of men!" Can I get a Hallelujah!

She describes the days leading up to the Republican National Convention in Minnesota thusly: "Eventually people started shuttling into the suite for introductions. Policy people. Communications people. Assistant people. Assistant-to-the assistant people. They were like human flashcards, there and gone."

Comparing the members of McCain's team to flashcards likens Palin's experience of learning the who's who of the McCain staff to cramming for an exam. And we all know how it feels to use flash cards to cram seemingly endless (often pointless) information into our heads: frustrating, exhausting, nerve-racking. Therefore, because of our own association with the word "flashcard," we also understand how the experience made her feel.

It probably made her sweat bullets. I know that's a cliché, but it just seems so apt when we're talking about Sarah.

Good metaphors allow readers to participate in a way that clichés do not. The readers' brains are stimulated to grapple with a connection between two things or ideas that they may have never considered before. They often also provide the readers with the opportunity to connect visually and emotionally to the material. But, of course, we don't want to bombard our readers with metaphors either. We don't want their brains to have to work too hard.

And, for that same reason, we don't have to completely avoid clichés either. As Jo Eberhart wrote in her article "In Defence of Cliches," "It's okay to throw in a pre-loved phrase every now and then. Clichés are shorthand for a whole language experience that ties into history, culture, and previously read stories." But if you are going to use one, please don't make it an eye-roller like "Sometimes life throws you a curve ball." Most important, don't overuse them because your voice gets lost. Using clichés is like plopping a Sarah Palin wig on your head. It's there. It's ready. You don't have to take the time to grow your hair out, or brush it, or tease it, or insert the (alleged) Bumpit. But it's not *your* hair. Why not find your own style that highlights your features? You needn't walk in someone else's Naughty Monkey Double Dare heels.

Chapter 9

Tone: Barracuda

Sarah Palin earned the nickname Barracuda during her high school basketball career. Some say it's because of the intensity with which she played the game. Others say it's because of the face she made due to that intensity—that "She [set] her teeth like she [was] eating jerky." But while all sources agree that when it came to playing basketball Sarah was intense, they don't all agree that she was good. Some say she was a star player, while others claim that she struggled. If the latter is true, she need not despair because there is one competitive sport that she must certainly excel at: the staring contest. I mean, the woman refuses to blink. She famously expressed her strict anti-blinking policy to Charlie Gibson in his 2008 interview when responding to his question about her reaction to McCain asking her to be his running mate:

> I -- I answered him yes because I have the confidence in that readiness and knowing that you can't blink, you have to be wired in a way of being so committed to the mission, the mission that we're on, reform of this country and victory in the war, you can't blink. So I didn't blink then even when asked to run as his running mate.

But she stopped blinking even before 2008. In her autobiography, she recalls being governor and sitting across the table from "well-heeled, lawyered-up oil executives" determining energy policy. She explained that during such negotiations, "You can't blink. And we didn't."

Palin may adhere to a strict anti-blinking policy, but she is certainly not averse to winking, as those of you who watched the vice presidential debate might remember. Sources disagree about the number of actual winks; some claim as many as six, others as few as three. I counted four.

; -) #1:

She winked in her response to Biden's point that at 9 a.m. McCain said the economy was strong and at 11 a.m. of the same day he said that they were in an economic crisis. She said the following:

> John McCain, in referring to the fundamental of our economy being strong, he was talking to and he was talking about the American workforce. And the American workforce is the greatest in this world, with the ingenuity and the work ethic that is just entrenched in our workforce. That's a positive. That's encouragement (WINK). And that's what John McCain meant.

That wink said, "We all know that's not what he meant, but, goshdarnit, I BSed that pretty good."

; -) #2:

The next wink came after moderator Gwen Ifill asked Palin if there was anything she has promised as a candidate that she'd have to take off the table because of the financial crisis, to which Palin responded thusly:

> There is not. How long have I been at this (WINK), like five weeks?

And that wink said, "Take that! I'm so inexperienced I haven't even had time to F up."

;-) #3:

The next wink came after Ifill explained that the biggest cliché about the vice presidency is that it's a heartbeat away from the presidency, so how would Palin deal with her and McCain's disagreements if, you know, McCain croaked. Palin responded by addressing the disagreement between her and McCain regarding drilling in Alaska's Arctic National Wildlife Refuge (ANWR):

> And heaven forbid, yes, if that would ever happen, no matter how this ends up, that that would ever happen with either party. As for disagreeing with John McCain and how our administration would work, what do you expect? A team of mavericks, of course we're not going to agree on 100 percent of everything. As we discuss ANWR there, at least we can agree to disagree on that one (WINK).

That wink said, "We all know that if John McCain kicked the bucket, I would totally drill, baby, drill."

;-) #4

And the last wink was just a shout out to her dad:

> I come from a house full of schoolteachers. My grandma was, my dad (WINK) who is in the audience today, he's a schoolteacher, had been for many years.

So her dad *is* a schoolteacher, but he *had been* for many years. Obviously, he didn't bring his work home with him.

But Palin's face doesn't just wink. It wrinkles its nose, it raises its eyebrows, it smiles profusely, it blows kisses. And the rest of her body gets in on the fun as well. Her pointer finger shoots up. So does her thumb. Her hand waves. Her head cocks. Her shoulders shrug. As Libby Copeland from the *Washington Post* described Palin, she's "extravagantly expressive." This, Copeland claimed, is how Palin connects so well with her audience.

It's what makes women imagine having coffee with her. It's what, as Copeland says, "allows her to leap through the camera into your living room." In fact, Palin's nonverbal communication is so strong that some believe it won her the vice presidential debate.

One of the challenges with writing is that without our body language we can't convey our tone—our attitude about the topic— as easily as we can when we're speaking. One of the reasons this can be a problem is because, as Sarah Palin would tell you, people are so doggone sensitive these days. Consequently, we pussyfoot around, we kowtow, we wear political correctness like a suicide vest, and what's worse, sometimes we even apologize. In fact, people are so sensitive today that they even get offended when we end sentences with periods in our text messages. That's right. Ending a period in a sentence is now increasingly considered aggressive. The less aggressive alternative has become either omitting any end punctuation or using a playful exclamation mark!

Another way we use punctuation to indicate tone is by surrounding the words and phrases we intend sarcastically in quotation marks. This can be helpful because sarcasm is particularly difficult to convey when not accompanied by the tone of our voice and facial expressions. Sarah Palin uses this technique quite a bit in her Facebook posts. For example:

Dear Congress:

Do your flippin' job and hold your chosen "leader" accountable for lying to a very concerned and fed-up American public. Make your guy set the record straight and publicly apologize for this. . . NOW. If not, your complicity in dealing with Lyin' Ryan screams of your approval of political deception and corruption has infested your whole lot, rotting Congress to the core.

Paul Ryan, with all his "lyin'"—whether that means he doesn't tell the truth or is often in a prone position—clearly is no kind of leader. Similarly, Obama and Hilary's policy is no policy:

Another reminder that Obama and Hillary's Iran "policy" is to wave the white flag and give them everything they want.

Obama's treaty with Iran, Sarah Palin claimed at a rally, would only bring victory or safety in a "world full of sparkly fairy dust blown from atop his unicorn as he's peeking through a pretty pink kaleidoscope." Since she believes that Obama's treaty with Iran would only work in a "world full of sparkly fairy dust," it's clear why she put policy in quotation marks; she obviously doesn't take it seriously. But, I don't know, the guy has his own unicorn; I might give him the benefit of the doubt.

It's one thing to signal to our readers that we are being sarcastic; it's another not to offend them with our sarcasm. Now, I'm pretty sure that Sarah Palin didn't care if she offended Paul Ryan, Barack Obama, and Hillary Clinton with her sarcasm in those Facebook posts. Nor do I think she cared if she offended Katie Couric with this post dripping with classic sarcasm: "Nahhh, Katie Couric would never edit an interview to make a conservative look bad." But for those of us who employ sarcasm for laughs rather than offense, thank goodness for Scott Fahlman. He's the guy who invented the emoticon. In 1982, on an online bulletin board at Carnegie Mellon University, he wrote, "I propose the following character sequence for joke markers: :-). Read it sideways." And that, my friends, is what Sarah Palin and the emoticon have in common: they were both around in the '80s, but no one heard of them until the 2000s and now they're flippin' everywhere.

The use of emoticons is definitely becoming more acceptable in the workplace. Studies show that over 70 percent of Americans have used emoticons at work. However, they're widely not considered appropriate for all work-related audiences—such as those elitist executives—and they're not considered appropriate for more formal types of work-related correspondence. And then, of course, there's the question of whether or not grown men should use them. Well, that's the question that was posed in the *New York Times* article "Should Grown Men Use Emoji?" One woman interviewed for the article said, ""If I'm seeing a guy, and he emojis, I feel uncomfortable. We're too old to be doing this. To have a man in his 40s and 50s using emojis is uncomfortable to me." A male CBS executive interviewed for the article agreed that emoticons are for the younger generation because they remind him of Taylor Swift, but he does use them sometimes because he believes, "If you're confident in your manhood, you can certainly lapse into Taylor Swift-hood momentarily."

Emoticons *are* a great way to channel our inner Taylor Swifts and to not offend our readers, but we certainly can't rely on them to convey our tone— and not just because the appropriateness of their use is debatable. It's because they can't sufficiently do the job of conveying our attitude about the content on the page. We need our readers to really feel if we are enthusiastic, passionate, concerned, angry, professional, or jovial about our material in a way that a smiley face, a sad face, or even a face with one eye winking, one wide eye and a tongue poking out can't communicate. So in order to effectively convey tone, we must rely on the English language, or the American language, as Sarah would say. And we need to rely on all of it: its nouns, its verbs, its adjectives, its punctuation, and its grammar in order for our written words to be as extravagantly expressive as Sarah Palin's face. In fact, Sarah Palin's written words are often as expressive as her face. For example, in the post about Lyin' Ryan, there's no mistaking how she feels. The Barracuda comes out gnashing her teeth. Let's have another look:

Dear Congress:

Do your flippin' job and hold your chosen "leader" accountable for lying to a very concerned and fed-up American public. Make your guy set the record straight and publicly apologize for this. . . NOW. If not, your complicity in dealing with Lyin' Ryan screams of your approval of political deception and corruption has infested your whole lot, rotting Congress to the core.

We already talked about her sarcastic use of the word "leader," so let's look at her word choice: "flippin'," "deception," "corruption," "infested," "rotting to the core"—clearly, she's not pleased. She also chose to write in the second person and directly address Congress, which conveys confidence and urgency. And she doesn't just talk to Congress; at one point she yells at them with her all-caps "NOW." Maybe the grammar error in the last sentence was intentional too. Maybe she wanted to show she was so enraged that she couldn't even calm down long enough to stick the word "that" between "corruption" and "has."

This post about Hillary Clinton also has the Barracuda bite:

> So Hillary's campaign stylist apparently leaked to the NYT she wore a white pantsuit to her convention as homage to the democrat female politician, Geraldine Ferraro, who'd also worn white. I was asked why I wore white, too. For the record - I wore it in '08 because it was the outfit with no baby barf encrusted on the shoulder.

Obviously, Palin thought it was silly of Clinton to wear white simply to honor Geraldine Ferraro. And why is it obvious? First of all, because she begins the post with the word "so" and uses the word "apparently," both which come off as condescending and confrontational. And, then of course, she compares Hillary Clinton's lofty, symbolic reason for wearing her white suit to Palin's own down-home, practical reason for wearing her white suit, which is meant to make Clinton seem artificial and pretentious. Palin emphasizes her own lack of pretention by using the very real image of "baby barf encrusted on the shoulder."

They must not have burp cloths in Alaska.

Now, note how Palin's tone changes when she posts about people she actually likes:

> Those with commonsense, concern, and tremendous love of country are pitching in and helping out the GOP nominee win for America. Thank you, Coach Mike Shanahan, for your boldness in supporting our next President. Denver was always blessed to have you, and now the rest of America benefits with your efforts to see Donald Trump fight for America. Coach Shanahan and DJT make a great team - they're in it to win it for the U.S.A!

Gone are the angry all-caps and the sarcastic quotation marks, the G-rated profanities, and the ellipsis because she's so mad she needs a sec to gather

her thoughts. Gone are the condescending words and blunt images of encrusted baby barf. Here, we have calm and collected complete sentences made up of professional, positive words, like "commonsense," "concern," "love," "helping," "boldness," "supporting," "blessed," and "benefits." It's like an angelfish ate the Barracuda.

And when she's posting about her family, the hockey mom tone takes over:

> oDarn! Tomorrow the calendar flips to August, meaning Alaska's summer starts winding down. My best buddies (my kids!) and I are soaking up a last week of sunshine before our back-to-school Autumn prep begins. It's been a great week away from work & politics - with Trig learning to swim like a fish! Ahhhhh, thoroughly enjoying my best buds amidst God's organic vitamin D.

Her "flippin'" has been mommified to a good ole "oDarn." And it looks like she plucked some enthusiastic exclamation marks out of her scrapbook. The dark world of infestation and rotting and yelling is gone, and the bright world of sunshine and swimming and long drawn out "Ahhhhhs" shines thorough. Even God made an appearance.

And in this post about going to a baseball game with her youngest son, Trig, we've got a couple of those exclamation marks, positive language, and an image of the American dream:

> On a date with Trig at the Rays vs D'backs game! Meeting great baseball fans and sitting in blessedly prime seats thanks to our friend Mike Ingram and his El Dorado Holdings team. Baseball, apple pie and motherhood - doesn't get any better than this living in the USA!

The only thing that could ruin this day is if Trig barfed apple pie all over her shoulder. Actually, I take that back; I'm sure she brought a spare $2,500 white Valentino suit jacket just in case.

And when she's trying to sell her motor home on Facebook, Palin takes on the tone of a used car salesman:

This is the perfect time for a road trip! Our family has enjoyed many of them - especially in this bunkhouse on wheels! Memories to last a lifetime in this beautiful rig; you can make your own positive, indelible memories in this motor home that we've enjoyed enormously. We've had to park our beloved Dynamax too far away from Alaska so decided to let it go to others who have that same bucket list item we have: loading up the crew, hitting the wide open road, truly experiencing America!

Being the largest state with the third smallest population, Alaska must not have had room for that old bunkhouse on wheels.

Sarah Palin wears her heart—or sometimes the lack thereof—on her sleeve. And this "strong emotional appeal," claimed linguist Eric Acton in an article in *Business Insider*, "is part of the reason she is such a provocative figure." Sarah Palin is so extravagantly expressive I think she deserves her own emoticon. It would be called the Barracuda. The eyes would be wide open, the teeth would be clenched, and there would be a little piece of jerky poking out of the mouth.

Chapter 10

Quotations: The Vetting Process

Hiring the same guy who vetted Sarah Palin to vet your vice presidential pick seems about as sound as hiring the person who designed the Titanic to design your luxury liner, but Donald Trump did. And to be fair, it's not like A. B. Culvahouse Jr., the attorney who vetted Sarah Palin, didn't realize Palin had shortcomings. He admitted that her lack of foreign policy and defense experience meant she would not actually be ready to be vice president on Jan. 20, 2009. But he believed she had "the presence and the wherewithal to grow into the position." So, ladies and gentlemen, do not forget to include presence and wherewithal in your résumé. Apparently, it can go a loooooong way.

But although the vetting caught Palin's lack of experience, it missed some important issues because the McCain team was frantic to find a VP. A few days prior to introducing Palin as his running mate, McCain *still* hadn't chosen a VP and, apparently, he offered Palin the job only moments after his first face-to-face interview with her. (As Madonna would say, Sarah Palin apparently "gave good face.") Because of the short notice, the McCain team assigned to vet Sarah didn't even arrive in Alaska until the day before she was announced. Consequently, they didn't vet her thoroughly as they probably should have. Also, they made some incorrect assumptions. McCain's senior campaign strategist and advisor explained that they assumed "that anyone with 'Governor' next to her name has a base level of knowledge of history and policy." So now they know; the next time they vet someone, sneak in a question about Paul Revere.

But before we get too judgmental about the McCain team's job of vetting Palin, let me ask you a couple of questions. Have you ever used the saying "Blood is thicker than water" to convey that family is more important than friends? Have you ever channeled Gandhi and said, "Be the change you want to see in the world"? Have you ever said in your throatiest voice "Luke, I am your father"? If so, then you did not properly vet your quotes before you employed them.

"Blood is thicker than water" is actually derived from the quote "The blood of the covenant is thicker than the water of the womb," which means that the blood shed by soldiers creates a stronger bond than the blood of the family. So it actually means the opposite of what most of us think it means. Gandhi didn't actually say, "Be the change you want to see in the world"; he said, "If we could change ourselves, the tendencies in the world would also change. As a man changes his own nature, so does the attitude of the world change towards him. . . . We need not wait to see what others do." But "Be the change you want to see in the world" does fit a hell of a lot better on a bumper sticker. And Darth Vader didn't actually say, "Luke, I am your father;" he said, "No, I am your father." So for over twenty-five years, every guy named Luke has suffered upon introducing himself because of this misquote.

And if anyone should know about suffering because of a misquote, it's Sarah Palin. Her tombstone will probably say, "I can see Russia from my house." But she didn't actually say that. Tina Fey did in one of her *Saturday Night Live* parodies of Sarah Palin. What Sarah Palin actually said was, "They're our next-door neighbors, and you can actually see Russia from land here in Alaska, from an island in Alaska." Granted, it's still not a great argument for foreign policy experience.

Sarah Palin was also misquoted by a group of Atheists. The American Atheists sponsored a billboard that quoted Sarah as saying, "We should create law based on the God of the Bible." But Sarah didn't say "should"; she said "would." Palin was discussing the National Day of Prayer and said, "I think we should . . . go back to what our founders and our founding documents meant. They're quite clear that we would create law based on the God of the Bible and the Ten Commandments." The president of the American Atheists may have been right when he argued that would/should, tomato/tomahto the "intent and context" of what they quoted her as saying is accurate—but it doesn't matter. We don't put quotation marks around words to convey intentions; we put quotation marks around words to let readers know that the words inside the quotations marks are the actual words that were said or written. Words inside quotation marks can't be tampered with in order to suit the writer's needs. Words inside quotation marks are sacred. Sorry, Atheists, I mean that words inside quotation marks are kind of a big deal.

I really hope that Sarah Palin was wrong and our laws aren't based on the Ten Commandments, not because I covet my neighbor's ox, but because I just lied about not being able to tamper with words inside quotation marks. We can, but we have to let the readers know. For example, the Sarah Palin quote in the previous paragraph includes an ellipsis (. . .). It's there because I put it there. I used it to indicate that I left words out of the quote. The entire quote is "I think we should kind of keep this clean, keep it simple, go back to what our founders and our founding documents meant. They're quite clear that we would create law based on the God of the Bible and the Ten Commandments." I omitted the part about keeping it clean and simple because it wasn't relevant to the point I was making, and because omitting those words didn't alter the meaning of her words. We can't just omit any old words from a quote. For example, it would not have been acceptable for me to modify it like this: "I think we should kind of . . . law." Even though I do think that would be an apt tagline for the daytime TV judge series Palin is reportedly working on.

Because Sarah is, herself, a victim of the misquote and an advocate for creating law based on the Bible, you might think she would follow the advice of Luke (the apostle, not the Jedi) and "Do to others what [she] would want them to do to [her]. Wait . . . before I go on, I want you to notice what I did there. I tampered with the quote again. What Luke actually said was "Do to others what you would want them to do to you," but my sentence would have been grammatically awkward if I left the quote untouched. If we must change a quote to make it work grammatically, we can, but we have to inform our readers by bracketing the changes. We can also use brackets around words we added to a quote for clarification. For example, I added brackets for clarification in this Palin quote: "I thought of a passage from the book of Jeremiah 29:11-13 [the prophet, not the bullfrog]: 'For I know the plans that I have for you,' declares the Lord.'" But, again, we can't alter anything that would distort the original quote's meaning. For example, if the American Atheists wrote, "We [sh]ould create law based on the God of the Bible," it still wouldn't have been kosher. Sorry, Atheists, I mean, it still wouldn't have been cool.

But, as I was about to say, even though Sarah Palin has suffered because she was misquoted, she freely misquotes others. For example, in her Trump endorsement speech, she misquoted Ronald Reagan when she said the following: "When we're talking about no more Reagan-esque power that, that, comes from strength. Power through strength. Well, then, we're talking about our very existence, so, no, we're not gonna chill. In fact, it's time to drill, baby, drill down, and hold these folks accountable." However, Reagan didn't say, "we're not gonna chill;" he said, "we're not gonna chillax," but since "chillax" didn't rhyme with "drill," Sarah changed it to "chill." I'm kidding, I'm kidding. Reagan's quote is "peace through strength," not "power through strength." In fact, Palin's quote of "power through strength" more closely echoes the sentiment of Darth Vader's code of the Sith ("Through strength I gain power") than it does Reagan's code of foreign policy. Did Palin join the Dark Side?

Judging from her response to Palin using her quote, Former Secretary of State Madeline Albright definitely thinks Palin joined the Dark Side. Palin told the audience at one of her rallies that it must have been "providential" for her Starbucks cup to host Albright's famous quote, "There's a place in Hell reserved for women who don't support other women." Albright's actual quote was "There's a special place in Hell reserved for women who don't help other women." But Palin's misquote was not what upset Madeline Albright. What upset her was the fact that Palin used the quote for political means when Albright said, "What I said has nothing to do with politics." Albright's words were meant to empower women at a WNBA luncheon in 2006. With this in mind, Albright blasted Palin for using her quote , saying:

> This is yet another example of McCain and Palin distorting the truth, and all the more reason to remember that this campaign is not about gender, it is about which candidate has an agenda that will improve the lives of all Americans, including women. The truth is, if you care about the status of women in our society and in our troubled economy, the best choice by far is Obama-Biden.

Apparently, there's also a special place in hell for former governors who use quotes for political gain that were meant to empower and unite women.

Speaking of Hell, Sarah Palin posted on Facebook that she was not just saying "no" but "hell no" to Obamacare. She believed that Obamacare included "death panels" that evaluated the elderly's "level of productivity in society," and would revoke their Medicare if they were found unproductive. (That's why I made my grandma start mowing my lawn.) With such a reverence for Medicare, it's strange that at the end of her vice-presidential debate Palin quoted Ronald Reagan thusly:

> It was Ronald Reagan who said that freedom is always just one generation away from extinction. We don't pass it to our children in the bloodstream; we have to fight for it and protect it, and then hand it to them so that they shall do the same, or we're going to find ourselves spending our sunset years telling our children and our children's children about a time in America, back in the day, when men and women were free.

It's strange because Reagan said this in order to persuade people to oppose Medicare in a campaign called Operation Coffee Cup. During the late

1950s and early 1960s, the American Medical Association had doctors' wives organize coffee meetings to convince their guests to oppose Medicare. In 1961 Ronald Reagan created an LP record called *Ronald Reagan Speaks Out Against Socialized Medicine*, and the record, which included the quote Sarah Palin used, was played at these meetings. So basically Palin used a quote that was originally meant as a preemptive death panel. She really shouldn't mix her quotes and coffee.

But at least Ronald Reagan said what Palin said he did—because Gandhi didn't. Palin posted a picture of Trump on Facebook with the following quote attributed to Gandhi superimposed on it: "First they ignore you, then they laugh at you, then they fight you, then you win." But Gandhi never said that. What was she thinking? Not about misattributing the quote to Gandhi; many people, including Bernie Sanders and Hillary Clinton, have done that. But how could she compare Trump to Gandhi? They couldn't be more opposite. Britain fought to keep Gandhi from breaking free from Britain, while over 500,000 Brits signed a petition to keep Trump out.

Palin also misattributed a quote to Thomas Jefferson—twice. In her 2015 Iowa Freedom Summit speech, a speech that was widely considered a sign she was considering running for president in 2016, she claimed that Jefferson warned, "When the people fear their government, that is tyranny. When the government fear the people, there is freedom." If that quote is true and Palin did run for the presidency, many might have perceived her bid as a potential precursor of tyranny. Also, in an interview with Katie Couric, Palin claimed that Jefferson said, "Never underestimate the wisdom of the people." (McCain's vetting staff might argue the opposite.) However, neither of those quotes can be attributed to Thomas Jefferson. A Jefferson quote that would have really come in handy, though, during her Katie Couric interview is "The man who reads nothing at all is better educated than the man who reads nothing but newspapers."

But I do understand why she was so eager to quote Thomas Jefferson; she wanted to make up for the answer she gave Glenn Beck when he asked her to name her favorite Founding Father. At first, she answered as though the Founding Fathers were newspapers: "You know, well, all of them." But Beck insisted that she choose one, and so she settled on

George Washington because, as she explained, he returned power to the people and was reluctant to serve. If you ask me, though, I think it's because he was the hot one. But even though Palin did ultimately name George Washington, the vagueness of her first answer caused her to be ridiculed for not really knowing the Founding Fathers. So, I imagine the Jefferson quotes were her way of saying, "You betcha I know them."

And to really prove she knew her Founders; she included a quote in *Going Rogue* by a more obscure Founding Father, Thomas Paine. She wrote, "When the next boom came during my administration, we were determined to be conservative and accountable to future generations." (As Thomas Paine said in 1776: If there must be trouble, let it be in my day, that my children may have peace.) The good news is that Thomas Paine did actually say that. The bad news is that the quote is like Cinderella's evil stepsister trying to cram her foot into the glass slipper; it doesn't quite fit. The "trouble" Paine was referring to was war; the "trouble" Palin was referring to was experiencing an economic boom. If an economic boom is trouble, sign me up. But I do get where she was going with it: like Paine, her administration was going to make sacrifices so the next generation could thrive. However, Paine and his generation would be sacrificing their lives; Palin and her administration would be sacrificing, perhaps, a new hockey field or a bridge to nowhere.

Bridge building presumably had been put on hold during Palin's first two—I mean, only two—years as governor, but I imagine fence building didn't dwindle. Palin likes fences. In 2010, she posted a quote from Robert Frost's poem "Mending Wall" on Facebook: "fences make for good neighbors." (Well, the actual quote is "good fences make good neighbors.") She posted this quote in response to the news that a man writing a book about her would be moving in next door. She followed the quote with, "Well, we'll get started on that tall fence tomorrow." (And had it been five years later, she might have been inspired by her buddy Trump to follow that up with "And we'll get him to pay for it.") But Frost's poem doesn't advocate that neighbors isolate themselves from each other by building fences; in fact, it argues the opposite. Frost intended the neighbor in the poem who says that "good fences make good neighbors" to represent an outmoded way of thinking.

According to writer Dudley Nichols, "Fear is the highest fence," and I hope this chapter doesn't make you scurry up that fence and become fearful of using quotes in your writing. Quotes are great. Quotes from experts can enhance your writing's credibility. Quotes from a voice familiar to your reader can help your reader connect to your writing. Quotes unfamiliar to your reader can enrich them. And quotes can help you when you're too lazy to come up with your own words. In other words, quotes have presence and the wherewithal to succeed. But before you copy and paste a quote from one of those websites, make sure you put it through the proper vetting process. Make sure you attribute it correctly, double-check the context, make sure it fits with your context, and that you understand it well enough to employ it correctly. Quotes are misused all the time, and you don't want to be part of the problem. As Gandhi didn't say, "Be the change you want to see in the world."

Chapter 11

E-mail Etiquette: Always Wear Clean Underwear

The name Sarah Palin evokes many things for many people, one of which is most likely not Latin scholar. Okay, maybe scholar is a little strong, but Palin certainly loves to dabble. One of her favorite Latin phrases seems to be *status quo*, which she even translated in her Iowa Freedom Summit speech for those of us not as well-versed in the classical Indo-European language. Apparently, it means "Man, the middle-class every day Americans are really getting taken for a ride." She also repeatedly uses the word *incognito*, which is derived from the Latin *incognitus*. But I think she has that translation backwards. She claimed she wore a blue sun visor on her Hawaiian vacation in an effort to be "incognito," which means to remain anonymous. This visor, however, had a giant black spot in the middle where she had blacked out the name John McCain, which, consequently, drew attention to the visor and, ergo, to her. Maybe she thinks "incognito" is Latin for "Man, I was John McCain's running mate, and all I got was this lousy visor."

Well, Sarah, I've got another Latin phrase for you to add to your collection: *semper ubi sub ubi*. It's a pun. When written it reads, "Always where under where," but when it's spoken it sounds like "Always wear underwear." Get it? The Latins are hilarious! Actually, if I were to share this phrase with Sarah Palin, I would slightly modify it to *semper ubi purus sub ubi*, and then I would wink knowingly at Sarah. My modification would translate as "always wear clean underwear," and Sarah would understand that I didn't mean this literally but as an analogy based on what happened to her e-mails. Like it's important to wear clean underwear because, God forbid, you get in an accident and end up at the doctors wearing dirty underwear (how embarrassing!), it's important to make sure your e-mails are spotless in case they get hacked by the son of a Democratic state representative.

Like many a celebrity, Palin's e-mails were hacked back when she was governor, and thousands of them were released for public consumption. And get this: she actually praised Obama! She said he gave a great speech. She also secretly had a tanning bed installed in the governor's mansion, which I totally understand. Alaska gets six months of winter. Surely, she didn't want to be known as Governor Pale Palin or the butt of an "Our Governor's So White" joke, like "our governor's so white she's whiter than the Republican base." Ouch!

Speaking of ouch, e-mails, themselves, can be pretty painful. That's because e-mail was thrust upon us like the vice presidential nomination was thrust upon Sarah Palin. It was a whole new world with a whole knew set of expectations that we were expected to navigate masterfully, yet we had never really been thoroughly prepared for. Like Sarah Palin was all of a sudden expected to know foreign policy, domestic policy, and which newspapers she read; we were all expected to confidently navigate all the ins and outs of e-mail. So although it sucks for Sarah Palin that her e-mails got hacked because now we all know she's not a natural bronze, it's good for us. Examining the e-mails she sent and received imparts important lessons that should help us navigate the treacherous world of e-mail.

Be a Straight-Shooter

Back in 2014, Sarah's eldest daughter, Bristol Palin, was involved in a drunken brawl at a snowmobile party. Bristol reportedly punched someone in the face five or six times—hard. In response to her daughter's behavior, Sarah Palin was . . . proud. In a Facebook post following the fight, Palin praised her daughter as a "straight-shooter" and one of the "strongest women you'll ever meet." Not that any of us are surprised by Sarah Palin's endorsement of aggressive behavior. Back on the night most of us first met her, the 2008 Republican National Convention, she told America that she was fierce. She described herself as a hockey mom and explained that the only difference between a hockey mom and a pit bull was lipstick. And she hasn't disappointed. In fact, if Sarah Palin were an e-mail, her subject header should be "Lipstick Wearing Pit Bull" because the job of an e-mail subject header is to accurately and succinctly introduce the e-mail's content.

One of the most common subject header errors is that they are not accurate; they are vague. A vague subject header would be akin to Sarah introducing herself as "an animal wearing makeup." We wouldn't know what to expect. Is she a moose wearing rouge? A zebra wearing foundation? A pig wearing lipstick? I'm sure you have all received an e-mail titled something vague like "Question" or "Hey" or "Meeting," which is frustrating because you are busy and it makes it impossible to prioritize its importance based on its subject.

A vague subject header is the issue with an e-mail Sarah received from her aide and friend, Ivy Frye. Ivy sent Sarah Palin an e-mail on April 30, 2008 with the subject header "Random." If I were Sarah Palin and I saw this subject header, I know what I'd be thinkin': "Goshdarnit, Ivy, I'm governor of the great state of Alaska. I receive hundreds of e-mails a day. I just gave birth to my fifth child. I've got a tanning session scheduled in twenty minutes. I need a random e-mail like I need a piece of tofu."

Let's have a look at Ivy's e-mail to see if he could have come up with a more effective subject header:

Incase we don't tell you enough already we love ya . . .

It of course goes w/out saying, but we'll continue working hard for you, and w unwavering support, to keep moving your awesome vision for Alaska forward.

On another note . . . it's a beautiful night–had an awesome run. I'm ready for you to be my running buddy–i figure if you're pushing the baby in a stroller we'll go the same speed.

See you tomorrow . . .

Of course, it goes w/out saying, that I have concerns about Ivy's e-mail in addition to its subject header, such as his refusal to write out the word *with*. What are you, Ivy, a commitment-phobe? And why so many ellipses, Ivy? Why not a simple period—or even an enthusiastic exclamation point—after "we love ya." A comma would have worked so much better after "On another note." An ellipsis indicates a hesitation, a trailing off thought, or suspense, so when you use an ellipsis after "See you tomorrow," it seems almost a little ominous, like "see you tomorrow . . . if tomorrow ever comes. Dun dun dun!" Are you threatening the governor, sir? Or are you using ellipses to mask your inability to punctuate properly? Are you a punctuation-phobe? And that little lowercase "i;" I know you're just an aide, Ivy, but we're all equal; you deserve a capital "I." Do you suffer from low self-esteem? Oh, and "in case" should be two words. But let's get back to that subject header.

The fact is that this e-mail is not as random as the subject header leads us to expect. "Random" indicates that the e-mail has no identifiable purpose, but it does; it has two purposes. The first is to express love and support to Sarah and the other is to inform her about the great run Ivy had. So Ivy could have, for example, titled his e-mail "Love and Running" or "A Great Governor and a Great Run" or "Loyal Aide and Running Buddy" or something like that. Those subject headers are more accurate, more engaging, and sound a lot less like a thirteen-year-old girl than "Random."

But that's not what I would have done. If I were Ivy, I would have taken a good hard look at my e-mail before sending it and asked myself an important question: WTF? And, of course, WTF stands for "What's the

Focus?" I would realize that e-mail's purpose is to express love and support to Sarah, so I would ask myself why I even included the running part because it detracts from the e-mail's main message and makes it about me. I would also realize that it kind of sounds like I am kissing her ass by drawing attention to that fact that she is a faster runner than I am. And then I would highlight that whole running part and click "delete." *Then*, I would return back to my subject header and title it either "We Love Ya," or "We Support You," or "Your Awesome Vision," or something like that.

You might think I am being too hard on Ivy. I mean, what's the big deal, right? It's just a little side note about running. Let the guy bond with his governor. Okay, *fine*. In friendly e-mails like Ivy's, it's not as crucial to ensure that the subject header indicates the scope of the e-mail content, but it *is* crucial if the e-mail contains information that the recipient might need to access at a later time. For example, the information in this e-mail sent to Sarah Palin from her aide Erika Fagerstrom titled "Tbed and Plmbg":

> *Hello,*
>
> *Sorry the beds not ready to go!!*
>
> *Here's an update:*
>
> *–AK Club will install a timer since the remote system used by the club doesn't work for home use–per Gail.*
>
> *–Rewiring bid for 220 outlet will be Monday 11/5 to include Todd's office as first choice. With the ceilings/walls up it makes it much easier.*
>
> *–The bed is up in the cedar closet, sorry I didn't realize it took a 220 outlet. As soon as we get a spot, we'll put it together and clean it up.*
>
> *The plumbing contractors re-worked the schedule to get the 2nd floor finished ASAP. I'll send you and Todd the new schedule on Monday.*
>
> *I turned the heat up–please let me know if the temp. needs to go up any more. The 1st fl. thermostats are in the 1st fl. hall closet.*

The subject header promises that the e-mail will be about the Tbed (which is short for the infamous tanning bed) and the Plmbg. (which is short for plumbing because governor's aides are so busy secretly installing tanning beds that they don't have time to write out entire words). And the e-mail is largely about the tanning bed and the plumbing. BUT . . . then we get to the last paragraph, and it's not about the Tbed or the Plmbg; it's about the heating—I'm sorry, the htng. So let's say that Sarah's skin is hot from a tanning session and she wants to turn down the thermostat, but she can't remember where it is. She receives thousands of e-mails a day; surely she doesn't remember which one contains the information about the thermostat. Now, she'll have to sift through all of them, which is going to take time away from her gubernatorial duties and, therefore, waste tax payers' money. Nice job, Erika. What Erika should have done is titled the e-mail "Tbed, Plmbg. and Htng." or sent a separate e-mail about the htng.

Ivy and Erika could learn a little something about how to properly execute a subject header by studying the following gems:

Invite – KRSA Reception Wed, 4/25 @5:00

A lesser subject header writer would have just titled this e-mail "KRSA Reception," thus requiring Governor Palin to take the time to open the e-mail to see if she can fit the reception into her busy schedule. But not this subject header maven. He or she knew the busy governor of the great state of Alaska would greatly appreciate a subject header that included all the information she needed to ascertain whether or not she could make it to the reception so she wouldn't have to waste precious tanning time opening the email.

Update on Rock Creek Mine in Nome

I love this subject header because it's as if the writer knew about Sarah Palin's challenges with geography. There is only one Rock Creek Mine in Alaska, but the writer took the time to specify its location, just in case. But what I really appreciate about this subject header is that it includes the word "update" to specify its purpose. A lesser subject header writer would have simply titled this e-mail "Rock Creek Mine."

I was not informed about Pt. Thomson and may be asked in tomorrow's press conference

This subject header was penned by Governor Palin, herself. Now, she could have just titled it "Pt. Thomson," assuming an e-mail sent by the governor would have enough clout to be opened immediately. But it's as if she saw her Katie Couric interview in a crystal ball and took the time to communicate the urgency of the situation in the subject header.

Now, I know that these subject headers are not sexy, but e-mail experts Mail Chimp found that the subject headers with the highest opening rates are "pretty straightforward." They simply tell the recipient what is actually inside the e-mail. They aren't "salesy, pushy, or slimy." They are like Bristol Palin: they're straight shooters.

Stop Pussyfootin' Around

Sarah Palin has what my grandmother would call *chutzpah*, or what Sarah Palin would call golden wrecking balls. It takes a lot of *chutzpah* to claim, like Sarah did in her autobiography, to have written funnier jokes for her appearance on SNL than the actual writers of *SNL* did, seeing as *SNL* has won over forty Emmy Awards. Sarah and her team came up with the idea that Sarah would pretend to be a journalist and ask Tina Fey (playing the role of Sarah Palin) condescending questions. The questions are as follows: "What do you use for newspapers up in Alaska—tree bark?" "What happens if the moose were given guns? It wouldn't be so easy then, eh?" And "Is 'you betcha' your state motto?" I am not as interested in the quality of the jokes as I am tickled by the fact that Sarah Palin is so proud of the jokes that she felt the need to share them with the world even though the SNL writers "smacked em' down."

Most of us are not that confident with the words we put out into the world. Consequently, many of our e-mails look like these that were sent to Sarah Palin:

I just thought I should tell you this interesting story.

I just wanted to drop you a note and say thanks for all you are doing for the people in Alaska.

I just wanted you to know also that as a single working mom I sure do appreciate the energy relief you proposed.

The strength of all these e-mails is diminished by the writers' inclusion of the word "just." In the context of these e-mails, "just" means "merely," which means that the writer doesn't believe what he or she has to say is that important. So if it's not that important, why even bother taking up the governor's time with it when she could be spending that time bouncing ideas off of SNL creator, Lorne Michaels. And if you don't believe in the importance of your writing, your reader most likely won't either. Note how much better the e-mails are when "just" is removed:

Before: *I just thought I should tell you this interesting story.*
After: *I have an interesting story to share with you.*

Now, there's that *chutzpah* I was looking for. I can't wait to hear your story. Please tell me it's about gun-packing moose!

Before: *I just wanted to drop you a note and say thanks for all you are doing for the people in Alaska.*
After: *Thank you for all you are doing for the people in Alaska.*

In addition to the "just," I edited out the part about "dropping a note" because it's redundant—if Sarah is reading the note, then it's clear that the writer wanted to drop it. Otherwise, he or she wouldn't have clicked "send." It's not like a moose had a gun to the writer's head.

Before: *I just wanted you to know also that as a single working mom I sure do appreciate the energy relief you proposed.*

After: *As a single working mom I sure do appreciate the energy relief you proposed.*

I deleted the "just wanted you to know" because if the writer hadn't wanted Sarah to know she wouldn't have written her. Unless . . . the writer was clairvoyant and knew that Sarah's e-mails were going to be hacked, and by "just" she meant "only," as in she only wanted Sarah to know, not the billions of people who would eventually have access to this e-mail.

I do understand why a lot of us use "just" in our e-mails. We are trying to be humble. We feel bad taking up our recipient's time. We don't want to sound brash. However, in order to be successful, it's important for your words to exude confidence. And think of it this way: whatever you have to say can't be any worse than Sarah's tree bark joke.

Reduce Your Carbon Fingerprint

With a base of hockey moms and Joe the Plumbers, it's clear that Palin identifies with the 99 percent. She does not, however, identify with the 97 percent—the percent of scientists that believe man is responsible for global warming. She said, "It's perpetuated and repeated so often that too many people believe that, 'Oh, well, if 97 percent of all scientists believe that man's activities are creating changes in the weather, who am I to question that?'" Being the maverick that she is, Palin not only questions it; she sides with the 3 percent of scientists who don't believe man is responsible for global warming. Her focus, therefore, is not on energy conservation, which is clear from this excerpt from one of her e-mails:

Kris, Karl:
    Pls set up a lunch or dinner with any/all former AGs. I've wanted to do this since my election:

Typing e-mails takes energy. Carpal tunnel isn't a tunnel in Nome, Alaska. But Palin only just barely gave a nod to the idea of energy conservation by conserving the energy it takes to type two *e*'s and one *a*. She does the same in this one:

> *And I just spoke to Matt Simon- basically wanted to know what I thot of the criticism on the radio that continues about Agia.*

Again, she conserves the finger energy it takes to type only three letters: *ugh*.

Speaking of *ugh*, that is a lot of people's reaction to using cyber speak, such as *pls* and LOL in work e-mails. On the other hand, it is becoming more commonplace. Hell, the executive branch of the government uses it. However, IMHO, there are a few things you should take into consideration. HTH (hope this helps):

- Make sure that your place of employment condones the use of abbreviations and acronyms in e-mails. Your employers have access to all your work e-mails; they don't even have to hack the system to get them.
- Dn't shrtn rndm wrdz. When Sarah Palin uses "thot," it's unclear whether it's an abbreviation or a spelling error.
- Buck up and use all your letters when you begin correspondence with someone new. It's respectful.
- Don't extend Sarah Palin's belief that "if you're in America, speak American" to "if you're on the computer, speak cyberspeak." If you're on the computer, you should still primarily speak American. Others might not be as fluent as you are in cyberspeak. Chances are your grandma thinks LOL means lots of love.

But again, shortening words doesn't really conserve that much energy. Plus, finger energy is only one kind of energy it takes to write e-mails; brain energy is another. Interestingly, 97 percent of scientists agree that the relationship between finger energy and brain energy is converse. In other words, the more finger energy we expel (i.e., the more words we type), the less brain energy we use. It's a lot easier to ramble off every idea that comes into our brains than it is to sift through those ideas and cull only the information needed by our readers.

For example, the writer of this e-mail seemed to use only 3 percent of his brain energy:

Dear Governor Palin,

Today the full House voted unanimously in support of the Purple Heart Trail Bill (SB216-HB293). Earlier the Senate also voted unanimously in support of the bill. I thank you for your support on the legislation and to my knowledge not a single person ever voted against it, not even during the various committee hearings. My two key supporters were Representative Berta Gardner and Senator Johnny Ellis, they both willingly stepped forward to get this issue through the legislative process, and now we have it, I am so very pleased with the results. We of course had many co-sponsors as well.

My question now revolves around the date that you will be able to sign the bill. Much will also depend on Berta Gardner and Johnny Ellis. I would certainly like for them to be present when you sign the bill. I am flexible and I will do whatever is needed to support your schedules. It is not mandatory that I be present, I would like to be but all will depend on your schedule and that of Rep. Gardner and Sen. Ellis. They have represented me extremely well and they can do so at any signing. They keep giving me credit for my work but I am absolutely convinced that this P/H Trail legislation would not have been accomplished without their dedicated involvement.

As you know we have invited you and your husband to our annual Department Convention banquet that will take place on the evening of May 3rd here in Anchorage. That would work for us but I anticipate a lot of interest from various veterans groups who may want to attend, but the location is probably not large enough to support the anticipated attendees. Maybe we could do it a different time that day (9am or so?) at the Anchorage Veterans memorial, that would hold any size crowd that may attend. 4 or 5 pm might also work that day because I think our convention will be over by around that time and everyone could simply head down to the Park Strip.

A second option may be on April 26th in Wasilla at "THE GATH-ERING" that will take place at 1 PM at the Wasilla Airport. One of the key event organizers (Ric Davidge) as well as myself hope to see you at that major veterans event if you can work it into your busy schedule.

We have no special favorites as to time or location and I am open to your schedule. I am even willing to jump on a flight to Juneau if I need to do so. I am just trying to find a date that will work for you and for us. We are simply anxious to see you sign this important and worthy deceased and wounded veterans legislation.

I anxiously await your reply and Thank You so very kindly.

I am, Yours in Patriotism;

Ron Siebels
MOPH, Alaska

Now, I don't know who Ron Siebels is. I don't know if he and Sarah Palin have a relationship that preexists this e-mail. I don't know if Sarah Palin has already agreed to sign the bill in question or if he's trying to persuade her. I do, however, know two things: 1) He really, really wants her to sign the flippin' bill. 2) Writing a long, rambling e-mail like this one is not the way to persuade anyone to do anything. First of all, it's terribly disrespectful of her time. If she has to read this whole thing, she's not going to have time to book her flight to Anchorage or Wasilla or wherever he wants her to go. Second of all, to paraphrase a quote widely attributed to Winston Churchill, the length of this might defend itself against the risk of being read. Sarah could conceivably take one look at this e-mail that lasts longer than an Alaskan winter and say "thanks, but no thanks" before even reading it.

Siebel's e-mail is 488 words long. I'm going to discuss it with him and see if we can get it down to something more reasonable:

Dear Governor Palin,

Today the full House voted unanimously in support of the Purple Heart Trail Bill (SB216-HB293). Earlier the Senate also voted unani-mously in support of the bill. I thank you for your support on the legis-lation and to my knowledge not a single person ever voted against it, not even during the various committee hearings. My two key supporters were Representative Berta Gardner and Senator Johnny Ellis, they both willingly stepped forward to get this issue through the legislative process, and now we have it, I am so very pleased with the results. We of course had many co-sponsors as well. Ron, you seem to be trying to convince Sarah of the bill's value, but she already supported it. It's all good, man! You can pretty much cut this entire paragraph.

My question now revolves around the date that you will be able to sign the bill. Much will also depend on Berta Gardner and Johnny Ellis. I would certainly like for them to be present when you sign the bill. I am flexible and I will do whatever is needed to support your schedules. It is not mandatory that I be present, I would like to be but all will depend on your schedule and that of Rep. Gardner and Sen. Ellis. They have represented me extremely well and they can do so at any signing. They keep giving me credit for my work but I am absolutely convinced that this P/H Trail legislation would not have been accomplished without their dedicated involvement. First of all, Sarah does not need to know about 97 percent of this paragraph's content. No offense, but she doesn't care about how badly you want Berta and Johnny there, or how well they represent you. Second of all, admit it, now you're just trying to show off. You not so subtly made it clear that you want Sarah to know that Berta and Johnny think you deserve all the credit. The first sentence is really the only sentence Sarah needs.

As you know we have invited you and your husband to our annual Department Convention banquet that will take place on the evening of May 3rd here in Anchorage. That would work for us but I anticipate a lot of interest from various veterans groups who may want to attend, but the location is probably not large enough to support the anticipated attendees. Maybe we could do it a different time that day (9am or so?) at the Anchorage Veterans memorial, that would hold any size crowd that may attend. 4 or 5 pm might also work that day because I think our convention will be over by around that time and everyone could simply head down to the Park Strip. Oh, Ron, I'm sorry, now I see what you're doing: you're channeling your inner James Joyce and writing in stream of consciousness: The Department Convention would work. Wait, no it won't because it's too small. 9 a.m.? No! 4 or 5 p.m.? Maybe! Maybe the convention will be over by then; maybe it won't. Are there any certainties in life? We're all just rolling stones. I love the Rolling Stones! I can't get no satisfaction.

A second option may be on April 26th in Wasilla at "THE GATH-ERING" that will take place at 1 PM at the Wasilla Airport. One of the key event organizers (Ric Davidge) as well as myself hope to see you at that major veterans event if you can work it into your busy schedule. It goes without saying that if she can't fit it into her busy schedule, she won't be there. Sorry, Ric. Here's a "k" if you want it.

We have no special favorites as to time or location and I am open to your schedule. I am even willing to jump on a flight to Juneau if I need to do so. I am just trying to find a date that will work for you and for us. We are simply anxious to see you sign this important and worthy deceased and wounded veterans legislation. Now, I am confused. You made such a big deal about having Berta and Johnny there, and now you don't care. What do you want, Ron???

I anxiously await your reply and Thank You so very kindly. Not as much as, I am sure, Sarah Palin anxiously awaited the end of this e-mail.

I am, Yours in Patriotism;

Ron Siebels
MOPH, Alaska

How about this:

Dear Governor Palin,

Thank you for your support of the Purple Heart Trail bill (SB216-HB283). Now that the Senate voted unanimously to pass the bill, I would like to arrange a time for you to sign it. Here are some possibili-ties:

- *April 26th at the Wasilla Airport at 1pm at the veterans event The Gathering.*
- *May 3rd at 9am or 5pm at the Anchorage Veterans Memorial.*

    If neither of these dates works, please let me know which dates work for you. I am even willing to jump on a flight to Juneau.

    I anxiously await your reply and Thank You so very kindly.

    I am, Yours in Patriotism;

Ron Siebels
MOPH, Alaska

That's a 77 percent carbon fingerprint reduction!

Have a Flippin' Point

In 2008 Sarah Palin was prank called by the Montreal comedians the Masked Avengers, who pretended to be French president Nicolas Sarkozy. They said some pretty crazy things to Palin, such as "I love the documentary they made on your life. You know Hustler's Nailin' Paylin?" and "You know my wife is a popular singer and a former top model and she's so hot in bed. She even wrote a song for you." On the one hand, it's hard to imagine that she thought that the president of France would say such things, but with her lack of foreign affairs experience, Palin may have just figured that that is how the French are.

But, I do have to say, her comebacks were pretty impressive. For example, when the Masked Avengers said, "We have the equivalent of Joe the Plumber in France. It's called Marcel, the guy with bread under his armpit, Palin just brought it right back to her talking points: "Right, that's what it's all about, the middle class and government needing to work for them. You're a very good example for us here." They also tried to poke fun at her "Russia" comment. "We have a lot in common also," they said, "because except from my house I can see Belgium. That's kind of less interesting than you." And, again, she remained unfazed: "Well, see, we're right next door to different countries that we all need to be working with, yes."

With such an ability to respond to seeming nonsense, I wonder how Palin responded to an e-mail sent to her by Paul D. Kendall. Kendall's e-mail wasn't a prank; it was worse—it was this e-mail with no discernible point or call to action:

Ladies and Gentlemen . . .

There are many journeys in place today and most of them are based on AWARENESS of various events, information, views, ideas, discussions and feelings . . .

I hope my comments and datas gathered are helpful and entertaining to you . . . IF they are not i will try to improve them. . . I have a lot of various articles to send you,, i thought you had people around you that most likely did this for you. . ...

I think this may be my (or one of my many) problems; I'm thinkin you have to be stupid or corrupted to make some or many of the decisions you have made lately,,,,now i think perhaps you just didn't know or have access to other developments in energy that are happening out there. . ...

So, i will try to forward some data packs to you. . .(while i am not being paid to do so) that others around you must not be doing.

Paul D. Kendall

Basically, what I get from this e-mail is that Paul is going to *try* to send some data packs. I guess Palin could just respond, "Good luck with that." But let's say that, against all odds, Paul succeeds: he mails the data packs. Then what? What is she supposed to do with them? Does he want her to apply the data to anything in particular?

Maybe Paul just wanted to vent. Maybe it felt good to tell the Palin administration that he thinks they're "stupid and corrupted," and maybe it was cathartic for him to communicate in grammatically incorrect sarcasm. Studies show, however, that e-mail venting (or e-venting) actually makes e-venters feel worse in the long run because they will likely reread the e-mail over and over again and dwell on it. And this was especially risky for Paul because he wasn't even sure he could mail the data packs as it was; with the extra time he spent dwelling on this e-mail, it's doubtful that he ever made it to the post office. Another reason that it was unproductive for Paul to send a hostile e-mail like this one is because calling Sarah Palin "stupid and corrupted" was most likely not going to compel her to open her mind to his concerns; it most likely compelled her to throw it in the e-trash. Therefore, this e-mail was perfectly pointless and a waste of time for the sender and the recipients.

I prefer this e-mail from one of Sarah Palin's aides. There's a touch of venting, but there's also a point:

> *After nearly tossing myself off the top of the Atwood, Andrew Halcro and I just completed a one-plus hour phone conversation — first, we spoke about the leak that he and the Governor discussed a job during the administration and perhaps his anti-AGIA rants are related to the fact that he didn't get the job. I reiterated the fact that this Administration had nothing to do with the leak (in case anyone caught talk radio today). Secondly, I discussed aspects of the AGIA and expressed my disappointment in him that he did not take up the gasline team on the opportunity to have an informational meeting to ask questions and discuss the merits of AGIA. We ended the meeting with the team regarding the AGIA and his concerns that we've not taken some things into consideration, especially in our cash modeling, etc. At this point, just filling everyone in, but would like to know what opportunities may exist for this conversation to take place.*

The writer of this e-mail got to vent a little about her interaction with Andrew Halcro, but she also let her recipients know why she provided the information that she did: she wanted everyone to know what she and Andrew Halcro talked about and she wanted to schedule a time to talk about Halcro's concerns. Great! Let's start throwing around some times and locations. Just make sure not to schedule at the top of a high rise.

Sometimes we don't want anyone to *do* anything with the information in the e-mail. When that's the case, it's also helpful to let the readers know that, like Sarah Palin did in this e-mail:

FYI – this is unprecedented. I believe, that litigation would be pursued re: our fisheries nominees. Just fyi for now.

It's a bit redundant that she wrote "FYI" twice, but I approve because her recipients don't have to wonder if they're supposed to do something with the information. As Palin would say, her e-mail is *verba non acta*, which is Latin for "words, not action."

Palin's enthusiasm for Latin was probably passed down from her Grandfather Sheeran. She shares his favorite Latin saying with us in *Going Rogue*: *"Illegitimi non carborandum!"* It means, "Don't let the bastards get you down." So when you log into your e-mail on Monday morning to find seventy-five unread messages glaring at you, *illegitimi non carborandum!* Sure, many of them may contain vague subject headers, lack confidence, ramble on and on, and have no discernible directive, but if you *plumbum exemple* (lead by example), the world of e-mail will improve *velocius quam lectus apricatus installare* (faster than you can install a tanning bed).

Chapter 12

The Writing Process: Intelligent Design

Rumor has it that Sarah Palin is in talks to host a reality show as a Judge Judy type of judge, which some find unsuitable because she doesn't have a law degree. I find it unsuitable because she committed a felony. In April of 2008 she forged a signature. And it wasn't just any old signature; she forged God's signature. She wrote a letter to her family that grappled with the joys and challenges associated with the impending birth of her son Trig, who was diagnosed with Down syndrome, and she signed it *Trig's Creator, Your Heavenly Father.* She was ridiculed by some for being so narcissistic she believed she could speak "in the voice of God." I don't agree with this assessment. I don't think the letter reflects a god complex. I just think it shows that Sarah's a huge fan of God. What do they say? Imitation is the highest form of flattery.

She also seems to imitate what she believes is God's creative process. She believes that "we came about through a random process, but were created by god." She doesn't believe in evolution; she doesn't believe that "human beings began as single-celled organisms that developed into monkeys who eventually swung down from trees."

Clearly! If Palin believed in evolution, that would mean that she believes that creation occurs by logically building on what came before. It would also mean that she believes in survival of the fittest. And based on the way she often expresses herself, it's clear that she doesn't believe in either of those concepts. Her ideas don't often build logically on the ones that came before. Rather, it's as though she drops all her ideas from an airplane as she's hunting wolves and expresses them in the order that they land. She doesn't seem to select only the fittest words and phrases; she includes even the unhealthiest, most inaccurate ones. Her creative process definitely aligns with the way she imagines God's to be: random. And now that I think about it, much like God spoke the world into existence, Palin often seems to speak her ideas into existence before even considering what she is going to say.

Many probably think that that's a good thing. That spontaneous, raw, unedited expression is more authentic, more honest, more heartfelt than heavily contemplated, heavily edited expression. But is it?

Think about it. There's been a time when you've been asked to write or speak about a topic, maybe for work, maybe for school, and it seems like it's going to be so easy. You know exactly what you want to say and how you want to say it. Hell, it's not only going to be easy; it's going to be brilliant. To me, the brilliant message that burns inside you is the authentic you.

But then what happens? You turn on your computer or open your mouth, and what comes out doesn't remotely resemble that beaming, golden light bulb in your head. Instead, it sounds like this:

That's why I say, I, like every American I'm speaking with, we're ill about this position that we have been put in where it is the tax payers looking to bail out, but, ultimately, what the bailout does is help those who are concerned about the health care reform that is needed to help shore up our economy, umm . . . helping the . . . uh, it's got to be all about job creation, too, shoring up our economy and putting it back on the right track. So health care reform and reducing taxes and reining in spending has got to accompany tax reductions and tax relief for Americans.

Surely, this answer to Katie Couric's question about the $700 billion stimulus package, which was described by one columnist, as "a vapid emptying out of every catchphrase about economics that came into her head," wasn't the best Palin could do at communicating her view. If she had actually prepared an answer, which her aids say she refused to do, instead of speaking off the cuff, perhaps she wouldn't have sounded so vapid.

Actually, there is nothing wrong with a vapid emptying out of the head. In fact, it's a necessary part of the writing process. As linguist Steven Pinker explains, "It's hard enough to formulate a thought that is interesting and true. Only after laying a semblance of it on the page can a writer free up the cognitive resources needed to make the sentence grammatical, graceful, and, most important, transparent to the reader." In other words, that laying out a "semblance of our thoughts," which might simply be an emptying out every catchphrase we know about our topic, is necessary to free up the other stuff, the good stuff. But it's only the first step; it's not the version that should be put out into the world. The final draft should look very, *very* different from the first draft. The purpose of the first draft is to provide us with the material to work with, and the final draft is the masterpiece that results from carefully molding that material.

Think of the difference between the first draft and the final draft as the difference between Sarah Palin's hair when she walks into salon and that fabulous updo she leaves with. And believe me, that updo didn't sprout effortlessly from her noggin. According to a *New York Times* article, her hair went through several drafts. She and her hairstylist "experimented with full bangs, side-swept bangs, clips, curls, twists and blond streaks." They would "try more warm, red and coppery highlights or more of a contrast with pale highlights, not to be severe but just more striking." Creating a masterpiece requires a process. It requires trial and error. It involves a lot of rinse and repeat.

So for those of you who have always considered yourselves bad writers because you can't seem to easily translate the brilliant idea in your head onto the page, I have good news for you: no one can. Not even writers. Not even Pulitzer Prize and Nobel Prize winner William Faulkner. He said, "At

one time I thought the most important thing was talent. I think now that
— the young man or the young woman must possess or teach himself, train
himself, in infinite patience, which is to try and to try and to try until it
comes right." In other words, writing doesn't necessarily take talent; it takes
a lot of practice and a lot of patience.

What does help is to find a writing process that works for you. Author
Bernard Malamud said his process was to write a piece three times: "once
to understand it, the second time to improve the prose, and a third to
compel it to say what it still must say." Author Susan Sontag admitted to
not writing "easily or rapidly." She said, "My first draft usually has only a
few elements worth keeping. I have to find what those are and build from
them and throw out what doesn't work, or what simply is not alive." Sarah
Palin's writing process for her autobiography was to hire ghostwriter Lynn
Vincent. The process that I propose is a four-step process, the description
of which Sarah Palin has ironically greatly contributed to:

Step 1: Drill, baby, drill

I want to introduce the first part of the writing process, which is freewriting,
by borrowing one of Sarah's famous phrases: "Buck up or stay in the truck."
In other words, I know that you will want to skip this part because you
think you are too busy to spend your precious time jotting down ideas that
no one will ever see. I know you would rather just get to the writing of the
actual document. But I'd like to remind you that linguist Steven Pinker—
a Harvard professor who has written over a dozen books, and, like Sarah
Palin, was named one of *Time*'s 100 Most Influential People—said that this
is an essential step.

I'd like to borrow another quote from Sarah to make my case for the
freewrite: "The fact that drilling won't solve every problem is no excuse
to do nothing at all." And what I mean by this is I know what you're
thinking—that there's no way that drilling down into the deep recesses
of your brain *before* you start writing your actual draft is going to get all of
the ideas out of your head that you're going to need because you're going
to come up with ideas as you go. And I also know that you're worried that

you'll just start rambling and many of your ideas will be silly or irrelevant. But I wants to remind you of something else that Palin said: "[Tax] dollars go to projects that have little or nothing to do with the public good, things like fruit fly research in Paris, France. I kid you not." But surely she was kidding about the fact that this research has nothing to do with the public good, because fruit fly projects in France may seem silly and irrelevant to American tax payers' needs, but the fact is that the research is related to finding a solution to a fruit fly threat to California olive trees—and California is the only US state to commercially produce olives. And we know Sarah: she wouldn't want to take jobs away from hardworking Americans. In other words, sometimes our ideas that seem silly and irrelevant turn out to be quite valuable. So drill, baby, drill.

Now, some of your writing is based primarily on research rather than your own ideas, so if that's you, I'd like to ask you to recall the answer Palin gave Katie Couric when asked what she reads to "stay informed and understand the world": "Um, all of 'em, any of 'em that have been in front of me over all these years." This is great because when we're researching, we want to give ourselves the time and the space to read as much as we can about our topic. We want to keep an open mind and explore our topic from every angle, not only the most obvious. We even want to explore material loosely related to our topic because sometimes connections exist that we are not even aware of. The more material we accumulate, the richer our final draft will be.

Step 2: The Main Thing

For this next step, I suggest that you call Donald Trump because, as Palin revealed in her Trump endorsement speech, "he knows the main thing." But if you can't get a hold of Trump, it's up to you to figure out your main point. To find your main point, analyze your freewrite or your accumulated research and figure out what your focus is—what it is that you want your reader to know. And once you figure it out, write it at the top of a blank sheet of paper. Then, underneath it, outline all of your points that you're going to use to support that main point. And Sarah has an outlining tip; it's what she told *Alaska Business Monthly*: "I've been so focused on state government, I haven't really focused much on the war in Iraq." That's right;

you focus on that main point and that point only. If the main point that you wrote at the top of the blank sheet of paper is about state government, then your outline shouldn't include points about the war in Iraq. If you have points to make about the war in Iraq or anything else besides state government, that's great; you have two options. One, you can save them and write a separate document. Or two, you can include them in the report on state government, but you have to revise that main point at the top of your page to let the audience know that they will also be reading about Iraq, or whatever other points you have added.

So how will you organize your points in the outline? It really depends on the topic. Perhaps, you will organize your paragraphs chronologically. Or maybe you will organize them in order of importance. But I want to remind you that audiences can be varied. Sarah Palin once gave a speech to an audience made up of farm families, teachers, teamsters, cops, cooks, rocking rollers, holy rollers, *and* full-time moms. Now, most of you won't write to *that* motley of a crew, but there are, for example, some of you who write proposals that will be read by both a business-minded audience and a technical audience. If that's you, as Sarah once said, there "are unifying values from big cities to tiny towns, from big mountain states and the Big Apple, to the big, beautiful heartland that's in between." In other words, start with the unifying values—the simple, non-technical information that both audiences can understand—so you don't lose your business audience immediately.

Step 3: The Meat

In her autobiography, Sarah Palin unabashedly professes her love of meat. "I eat pork chops," she wrote, "thick bacon burgers, and the seared fatty edges of a medium-well-done steak. But I especially love moose and caribou." And I'm sure that was her way of saying that she loves it when writing is fleshed out with lots of thick, fatty specific details. And in this step, you get to do that to your writing. You have your outline, so you know what you're going to write. Now, it's time to write your real first draft, the one that is starting to look like your final draft. The focus of this step is on specific details; you're still not worrying about making it pretty.

Step 4: The Stylist

And now it's time to make it pretty. And if anyone knows the importance of this step it's the woman whose makeup artist was the highest paid individual in McCain's campaign during the first half of October. So Palin obviously has some great advice for you. First of all, she once said, "We eat, therefore we hunt." In other words, for many of us our writing is our bread and butter. We write copy for our websites advertising our services. We write cover letters to get jobs. We write business proposals to procure financing. Therefore, in order to get the clients, the jobs, and the money, we have to hunt for those great words that make our writing vibrant and reflect our personal style. We also have to hunt for unnecessary words and bloated phrases to cut to make our writing concise. We have to scour the page for any grammatical errors, such as subject-verb disagreements or abrupt shifts into the second person. Another great piece of advice Palin gave is "Only dead fish go with the flow." In other words, instead of relying on old, used up clichés, hunt for opportunities to create your own, unique metaphors.

As Sarah Palin said, she is "one to believe that life starts at the moment of conception." That means that even though most of the lessons we learned in this book don't become relevant until the third or fourth step, the life of your writing begins the moment you conceive of the idea or have been given an assignment, and that makes the first two steps just as important. But Palin is surprisingly "not anti-contraception." In other words, she understands that writer's block stems from an abstinence only approach to writing, an approach that espouses the belief that we cannot sully the virgin white page with words unless they are words that we intend to commit to for the rest of our lives. An approach that often results in staring at a blank page anxiously because of the performance anxiety it induces. Instead of agonizing over the perfect way to start, the perfect way to structure a sentence, or whether or not to use a semicolon, just start emptying out all of your vapid thoughts. And keep going because you'll get to some good stuff. Remember, Palin's hairstylist could never have created that perfect updo from a bald scalp.

Acknowledgments

In honor of Sarah Palin, I will begin my acknowledgments page as she did in her autobiography: by acknowledging Sarah Palin. Thank you, Sarah Palin, for providing me with so much fun material to work with. Next, I would like to thank Jerrod MacFarlane from Skyhorse Publishing for thinking of me for this book. I had so much fun writing it. I'd like to thank my husband for promising to help me with whatever I needed so I could write this book—and for sticking to that promise. I'd like to thank my dad for all the fabulous feedback he provided. I'd like to thank my mom for encouraging my writing by constantly telling me how brilliant I am. (I respond well to flattery.) I'd like to thank my mother-in-law for babysitting Sweet Baby Rae so I could escape to the coffee shop and write. I'd like to thank my father-in-law for sparing his wife for weeks at a time so she could babysit. I'd like to thank Rae for napping every day. Without those naps, this book would not exist. I'd like to thank Owen Ela for shooting my author photo. And I'd like to thank my friends and family for always being so supportive of me and my writing.

References

"2010 Economy Changed Many Americans' Lives." *NPR.* 30 November 2101. Web. 28 September 2016.

Abadi, Mark. "Linguists Explain Why Sarah Palin Has Such an Emotional Connection with Her Audience." *Business Insider.* 31 January 2016. Web. 28 September 2016.

Barkhorn, Eleanor. "Sarah Palin Misinterprets Robert Frost." *The Atlantic.* 25 May 2010. Web. 28 September 2016.

Beckwith, David C., "United States in 2010." *Encyclopaedia Britannica.* 20 May 2016. Web. 28 September 2016.

Bobic, Igor. "Here's The Funniest Thing Donald Trump Has Said Yet." *Huffington Post.* 17 August 2015. Web. 28 September 2016.

Bobic, Igor. "The Lawyer Who Vetted Sarah Palin Will Do The Same For Donald Trump's Veep." *Huffington Post.* 19 May 2016. Web. 28 September 2016.

"Debate analysis: Palin spoke at 10th-grade level, Biden at eighth." *CNN.* 3 October 2008. Web. 28 September 2016.

Bumiller. Eilsabeth. "Palin Disclosure Raise Questions on Vetting." *The New York Times.* 1 September 2008. Web. 28 September 2016.

Copeland, Libby. "Shooting from the Hop, With a Smile to Boot." *Washington Post.* 1 October 2008. Web. 28 September 2016.

De Nies, Yunji and Linda Owens. "Rush Limbaugh Drops 90 Pounds." *ABC News.* 3 August 2009. Web. 28 September 2016.

Eberhardt, Jo. "In Defence of Cliches." *Writer Unboxed.* 4 June 2016. Web. 28 September 2016.

Evon, Dan. "First They Ignore You, Then They Vote for You?" *Snopes.com.* 1 March 2016. Web. 28 September 2016.

Frank, Thomas. "The Persecution of Sarah Palin." *Wall Street Journal.* 17 November 2009. Web. 28 September 2016.

"Full Transcript: Charlie Gibson Interviews GOP Vice Presidential Candidate Sarah Palin." *ABC News*. 23 November 2009. Web. 28 September 2016.

Gourevitch, Philip. "The State of Sarah Palin." *The New Yorker*. 22 September 2008. Web. 28 September 2016.

Haber, Matt. "Should Grown Men Use Emoji." *The New York Times*. 3 April 2015. Web. 28 September 2016.

Hale, Constance. "The Pleasures and Perils of the Passive." *The New York Times*. 30 April 2012. Web. 28 September 2016.

Hale, Constance. "The Sentence of the Miniature Narrative." *The New York Times*. 19 March 2012. Web. 28 September 2016.

Hall Robert, J. Wisniewski, and Chris Snipes. "The 5 Most Frequently Misused Proverbs." *Cracked.com*. 17 February 2013. Web. 29 September 2016.

Hoffman, Jan. "The Upshot on Palin and Her Updo." *The New York Times*. 12 September 2008. Web. 29 Septmeber 2016.

Jones, Jeffrey M. "Clinton Edges Out Palin as Most Admired Woman." *Gallup*. 30 December 2009. Web. 28 September 2016.

King, Stephen. *On Writing*. New York: Pocket Books, 2000. Print.

Knoblauch, Austin. "Sarah Palin mistakenly attributes quote to John Wooden." *Sports Now. LA Times*. 1 December 2009. Web. 28 September 2016.

Krugman, Paul. "Raising the white flag of surrender — to Medicare." *The New York Times*. 3 October 2008. Web. 28 September 2016.

Kuntz, Tom. "'Hopey-Changey' Alive." *The New York Times*. 18 June 2011. Web. 28 September 2016.

Lam, Bourree. "Why Emoji Are Suddenly Acceptable at Work." *The Atlantic*. 15 May 2015. Web. 28 September 2016.

Luo, Michael. "Top Salary in McCain Camp? Palin's Makeup stylist." *The Caucus. The New York Times*. 24 October 2008. Web. 28 September 2016.

Madrigal, Alexis C. "Sarah Palin Ran a Faster Marathon Than Paul Ryan." *The Atlantic*. 3 September 2012. Web. 28 September 2016.

Millstein, Seth. "Sarah Palin's 'Splodey' Quote Is the Latest Addition to Her Growing Lexicon." *Bustle.com*. 1 July 2016. Web. 29 September 2016.

Palin, Sarah." *Going Rogue: An American Life*. New York: Harper Collins, 2009. Print.

"Peyton Place." *Wikipedia*. Wikipedia Foundation, Inc. 21 August 2016. Web. 28 September 2016.

Pinker, Steven. "Passive Resistance." *The Atlantic*. November 2014. Web. 28 September 2016.

Pinker, Steven. "*The Sense of Style: The Thinking Person's Guide to Writing in the 21st Century.*" New York: Penguin Group, 2014.

Power, Ed. "Why it's always a good hair day for Michael Bolton." *Independent.ie*. 27 May 2014. Web. 28 September 2016.

Purdum, Todd. "It Came from Wasilla." *Vanity Fair*. 30 June 2009. Web. 28 September 2016.

Rosen, Yereth. "Alaska's tab for ethics complaints about Palin: $1.9 million." *Christian Science Monitor*. 9 July 2009.

Sarah Palin Uncut. Pacific Publishing Studio, 2011. Print.

Schapiro, Rich. "What's in the Palin children's names? Fish, for one." *Daily News*. 31 August 2008. Web. 28 September 2016.

Schlesinger, Robert. "Sarah Palin Sends Out Fundraising Appeal With Grammatical Error." *U.S. News*. 9 February 2010. Web. 28 September 2016.

Schnall, Marianne. "Conversation with Madeleine Albright." *Feminist.com*. 1 June 2010. Web. 28 September 2016.

"Shoe fans go wild for Sarah Palin's campaign trail peep-toe heels." *Daily Mail*. 15 September 2008. Web. 28 September 2016.

Strohm, Mitch. "What is Donald Trump's net worth? The answer may surprise you," *Bankrate.* 4 May 2016. Web. 28 September 2016.

"Subject Line Comparison." *Mail Chimp*. Web. 28 September 2016.

Weisberg, Jacob. "The Complete Palinisms." *Slate*. 7 September 2011. Web. 28 September 2016.

Weisberg, Jacob. *Palinisms: The Accidental Wit and Wisdom of Sarah Palin.* New York: Houghton Mifflin Harcourt, 2010. Print.

Wing, Nick. "American Atheists Hit Republicans With 'Go Godless' Billboards, Correct Sarah Palin Misquote." *Huffington Post.* 5 March 2013. Web. 28 September 2016